Figurations of Human Subjectivity

Gabriel Bianchi

Figurations of Human Subjectivity

A Contribution to Second-Order Psychology

Dear Wendy,
thank you for all
your inspiration and
support that changed my
life so significantly!

palgrave
macmillan

Cordially
Gabriel

March 2, 2023
Bratislava

Gabriel Bianchi
Institute for Research in Social Communication
Slovak Academy of Sciences
Bratislava, Slovakia

ISBN 978-3-031-19188-6   ISBN 978-3-031-19189-3   (eBook)
https://doi.org/10.1007/978-3-031-19189-3

This Palgrave Macmillan imprint is published by the registered company Springer Nature Switzerland AG.
The registered company address is: Gewerbestrasse 11, 6330 Cham, Switzerland

...the more selves we find within ourselves, the easier is to find common ground with other multiple, multitude-containing selves... Yet we live in an age in which we are urged to define ourselves more and more narrowly, to crush our own multidimensionality into the straitjacket of a one-dimensional national, ethnic, tribal or religious identity. This ... may be the evil from which flow all the other evils of our time. For when we succumb to this narrowing, when we allow ourselves to be simplified and become merely Serbs, Croats, Muslims, Hindus, then it becomes easy for us to see each other as adversaries, as one another's Others, and the very points of the compass begin to quarrel, East and West collide, and North and South as well. (Salman Rushdie, Languages of truth. Jonathan Cape, 2021, p. 207)

Acknowledgement

This book brings a critical reflection of my decades-long research within psychology which, however, often crossed borders to sociology and possibly other disciplines as well. And it expresses my lifelong frustration from narrow-minded, well-designed and carefully published studies which tell so little about the genuine core of us as human beings. Therefore, I took the courage to try to identify which segments from my research could be useful in this direction. With the aim to disclose the nature of our complex and complicated subjectivity—of who we are. And thanks to some excellent scholars, there exists already a niche in the psychology-library shelf to which I would like to tuck this modest book. It has the tag "second-order psychology." Of course, my thanks go to many of my co-workers and students during my whole professional life, especially to all the bright, rare, extraordinary personalities I have had the opportunity to meet and be inspired by, and, of course, to all reviewers of the manuscript. And, last-not-least, my thanks go to my wife Mira, who remains to act as the vigorous supporter of my efforts.

The writing of this book was supported by the Slovak Research and Development Agency under the Contract No. *APVV-18-0303*, as well as by VEGA Grant: *2/0035/21 Family Constellations Involving Biological and Non-biological Children.*

Contents

List of Figures

LIST OF TABLES

CHAPTER 1

Diversity of Human Subjectivity Served on a "Social Representations Tray"

Abstract This chapter is not merely the introduction; it is also the most important part of the book as it outlines the central message—I am trying to justify the idea that it is worth looking for more complex renderings of human beings. Subjectivity, which I defend here, is the answer to this conundrum. I admit to being strongly inspired by the Brown and Stenner (*Psychology without foundations.* SAGE Publications Ltd., 2009) conceptualization of second-order psychology and by scholars from outside psychology. Nonetheless, I strongly believe that the message is one that applies to psychology directly.

I have chosen to highlight the topic of subjectivity in psychology, despite the risk of it immediately giving the impression of redundancy and prompting reactions such as: "Psychology IS in its very essence, and more than any other discipline, THE science on subjectivity. So why all the excitement about subjectivity?" But the truth is that subjectivity has, throughout the history of social science and the humanities, mainly been addressed in philosophy. If we search for subjectivity psychology, we need to look only at the late twentieth and twenty-first century (perhaps with the

G. Bianchi, *Figurations of Human Subjectivity*,
https://doi.org/10.1007/978-3-031-19189-3_1

1

exception of Wilhelm Wundt and his efforts [1]). And even then, as Danzinger (1997) points out, the dominant efforts were fragmentary—aimed at the analysis of sensation, perception and memory. They may have considered these in depth, but they failed to integrate them. Subjectivity is based on the wholeness of our mental apparatus; in the modernist era efforts in psychology focused on "measurable" and "predictable" personality variables/traits. The best and easiest example is probably the Big Five "theory," which to this day remains an icon part of most psychological research. But however "solid" the five personality traits may be, they are not considered together to produce a holistic view of human subjectivity. At the end of the twentieth century we can observe the "reinvention" of emotions (Greco & Stenner, 2008). But even in recent psychological assets integrating diverse determinants of human action there is no direct reference to a theory highlighting the central essence of the human subject as a psychological entity.

In this book I try to defend the position that, despite the lack of psychological interest in human subjectivity, there is (1) plenty of evidence of diverse forms of psychological subjectivity, and (2) it is to the detriment of psychology that these are not considered as they may be useful in civilization enhancement efforts.

The central goal of this book—which is to focus attention on the psychological aspects and diversity of human subjectivity (by mapping certain forms)—is achieved by selective use of the epistemological instrument developed by Serge Moscovici (1961, 2001), known as the theory of social representations. But before explaining Moscovici's theory as applied to the search for subjectivity, I discuss the importance of analysing human subjectivity from the psychological perspective.

---

[1] W. Wundt does not consider psychology to be a science of the individual soul. Life is a uniform mental and physical process that can be considered in a variety of ways in an effort to identify the general principles, particularly the psychological and historical and biological principles of development. Wundt thought understanding the emotional and the volitional functions, in addition to cognitive features, was just as important as grasping the aspects of the psychophysical process in its entirety. The ten volumes of his *Völkerpsychologie* are: Language (Vols. 1 and 2), Art (Vol. 3), Myths and Religion (Vols. 4–6), Society (Vols. 7 and 8), Law (Vol. 9) and Culture and History (Vol. 10). Völkerpsychologie. *Eine Untersuchung der Entwicklungsgesetze von Sprache, Mythus und Sitte [Social Psychology. An Investigation of the Laws of Evolution of Language, Myth, and Custom, 1900–1920, 10 Vols].*

1.1   SUBJECTIVE INCLINATIONS TO SUBJECTIVITY...

I began thinking about human subjectivity from the psychological perspective in a "post-hoc" manner, while reflecting on my academic efforts over the four decades of my work in psychology research. Concentrating on subjectivity was certainly not my strategic life-plan. But when thinking today about my life's research, [2] and trying to maintain a suitable distance and "levity," the central concept I keep returning to when attempting to obtain an integral understanding of psychological research is subjectivity.

1.2   ...AND OBJECTIVE JUSTIFICATIONS

These thoughts inspired and encouraged me so I started digging into the authoritative psychological knowledge on the issue(s) of human subjectivity. All my life I have viewed subjectivity with suspicion. On the one hand there is the common-sense expectation that subjectivity has to be the main perspective in psychology: after all it is the discipline that focuses on the psyche—primarily an individual entity. On the other hand looking at the academic writing in (not only the mainstream) psychology one gets frustrated—for subjectivity is at best a marginal topic. The growing interest in subjectivity displayed in certain quarters in recent decades is aptly described by Curt (1994, p. 46):

> Meanwhile, the question of the "subject" has become central to other areas of scholarly analysis. These include cultural studies, media studies, radical sociology, feminist psychoanalysis, art history, critical legal studies and literary studies. All of them have developed sophisticated post-structural, post-phenomenological approaches in order to address "the subject". What is notable is the extent to which such approaches have been largely ignored by mainstream psychology.

---

[2] Over my career, my PhD research focused on the individual (subjective) capacity for prosocial behaviour in children. I then (dis)continued with subjective thinking of the value of the environment and the subjectivity of environmental risks (e.g. Bianchi & Rosová, 1992; Rosová et al., 1989, 1996, 1998); through cultural subjectivity reified in the conceptualization of universal human values and its links to diverse aspects of political and civic behaviour; then, for several decades, I focused on sexual, intimate, coupledom and parenthood subjectivity; followed by various group subjectivities (gender and intimate citizenship); and finally human enhancement subjectivity (work in progress—Bianchi, 2019, not included in this book). Most of my research involved epistemological and methodological challenges.

But still, an emblematic piece of work has to be mentioned here. The originally published book *Changing the Subject* by Julian Henriques, Wendy Hollway, Cathy Urwin, Couze Venn and Valerie Walkerdine in 1984 raised its voice to fight for the need of focusing on human subjectivity and offered a strong and diverse argumentation for it—covering areas from the very subject of psychology per se, through organizational psychology, gender related subjectivity, power relations and language, racism and politics, to child-centred pedagogy. The complex explanation of the purpose of writing this book focuses on The Three critiques are the critiques from Henriques et al. "the notion of a unitary, rational subject … still predominate(s) in the social sciences in spite of the critiques which have shown such a concept to be untenable. These critiques have been developed from three standpoints, namely, critical theory and poststructuralist interrogations of the foundations of the discourses of modernity, feminist challenges to the phallocentric and masculinist model of subjectivity privileged in Western theory, and the 'postcolonial' questioning of the affiliations of the logocentric notion of the subject with the ideologies of racism and imperialism"[3] (Henriques et al., 2005, p. IX). To express the purpose of the book simply, let's take the following quote:

> The intention of Changing the Subject was [and still remains[4] due to the resilience of the cognitivist paradigms, the rationalist, logocentric notion of the subject in the mainstream psychology] to point towards recognition of **the complexity of the relation between culture and the psyche in the production of subjectivity and identity** (emphasis added). (Henriques et al., 2005, p. X)

A kind of spontaneous continuation of this book can be seen in the platform launched in 2008 by Lisa Blackman, John Cromby, Derek Hook, Dimitris Papadopoulos and Valerie Walkerdine—the Journal *Subjectivity*[5]— with the following justification:

---

[3] It should be acknowledged that the original manuscript of the book was designed in a historical era of emerging neoliberalism that can be called the times of the new right.

[4] The book, still relevant to the psychology and social sciences scene today—after almost 40 years from its origin, was successfully reissued in 1998 and electronically published in 2005.

[5] The journal was created by rebranding the *International Journal of Critical Psychology*. This change in subjectivity of the journal opens several questions (Has critical psychology gone out of fashion? Has ontology (of subjectivity) become more important than epistemology (of critical theory)? Or was it necessary to go beyond psychology and open up the whole arena of the social sciences and humanities to understand human subjectivity?) In any case, it would be a good subject for (a different) analysis.

The journal will bring together scholars from across the social sciences and the humanities in a collaborative project to identify the processes by which subjectivities are produced, to explore subjectivity as a locus of social change, and examine how emerging subjectivities remake our social worlds. (Blackman et al., 2008, p. 1)

They define (indirectly) subjectivity in this introducing editorial as follows:

subjectivity, which we could call the experience of being subjected... Subjectivity...is the experience of the lived multiplicity of positionings. (Blackman et al., 2008, p. 6)

The role of psychology in this effort—in contrast to all other social sciences and humanities exploring subjectivity—was apparently expected as the most marginal as it is named as the last:

As topic, problem and resource, notions of subjectivity are relevant to many disciplines, including cultural studies, sociology, social theory, science and technology studies, geography, anthropology, gender and feminist studies and psychology. (Blackman et al., 2008, p. 1)

In fact, however, the breadth of the journal's sensibility for uncovering and analysing subjectivity is fascinating, and psychology plays a not insignificant role in it. Here is the overview of the topics covered in papers in just three recent volumes of *Subjectivity*, it is literally breathtaking (see Frame 1.1):

Frame 1.1 Journal Subjectivity, Since 2008, Overview of Paper-Topics from Recent Three Volumes 13–15 (2020–2022)

2022 (issue 1–2):

- *Cultivation of the subject and enacting subjectivities via a yoga practice* of learning to feel as a tool for adjustment to conditions of precarity in everyday lives
- Understanding *emergence of mass-hysterical subjectivity* accompanied by bizarre and extreme behaviors due to affective contagions spreading through social-network assemblages

(*continued*)

Frame 1.1 continued

- *Logistics (processes of distributing merchandise) as a field where processes of subjectivation can be observed*, but also as the framework for the theoretical analysis of processes of subjectivation in contemporary consumer societies.
- *Dreams (approached psychoanalytically) are a relevant terrain for the study of contemporary subjectivities* at the service of social research
- *Constant pressure for young people to optimise themselves, to become the masters of their lives and to enjoy life to the full*, instead of leading towards a new empowered citizenship, amidst a world permeated by identity politics, *means a great challenge to subjectivity* which can be understood by a Hegelian philosophical interpretation.

2021:

- *Drug use's contribution to subjectification*; "affective technologies" to modify hegemonic narratives on subjectivity
- The *production of subjectivity in the clinical space as a political process* in the case of muscular dystrophy.
- How *migrants', refugees', and minority subjects' positions* are affected by the experience of colonialism and dislocatedness – *the disidentified subjectivities*
- Better understanding of *subjectivity exposed to the precipitation of memory and affect challenges* in the context of *post-colonial reflection of war and dominance*.
- *Community theater as a space for* community building labour facilitating *intersubjective becoming* during convivial encounters that are not based on a shared history
- *Abjection, space and resistance as subjectivity influencers in asylum seekers, migrants, as well as protesters against state-power-control*
- *Permanence and singnificancy of uncertainty of entrepreneurial future—a mode of subjectivity*

(*continued*)

- *Subjective experiences of synchrony or asynchrony with other rhythms and temporality present in the social environment, resulting in a certain capacity to plan one's life and overcome social stratification*
- How *childhood memories serve as a rich resource in formations of (middle-class) women's maternal subjectivity*
- *Threats to subjectivity in educational context: how a strategic effort to disrupt 'old praxis'* (introduction of flexible timetables into teaching practice) *can unleash turbulent emotional potentials of 'liminal affectivity' and transform and change teacher's professional subjectivity by disturbing their equilibrium*
- *Shaping of subjectivity within the process of research interviews on sexual victimization*

2020:

- A special issue consisting of six papers presenting work of the multidisciplinary and international *Affective Archives Research Group* reflecting on multiple *intersections between the affective and aesthetico-political as they occur at various global sites and impact upon various instantiations of subjectivity (in movie, painting, cartography, political biography and autoethnography)*
- *Rankings of scholars are - an apparatus of social transformation for the production of more governable subjectivities* for capital
- *Subjectivity of the ambivalent tensions between human and non-human, dominance and subordination*
- *Possibilities and challenges of bringing homo politicus back into the agenda of education*
- *Interactions of nationalism and populism at the creation of political subjectivity*

In accordance with my intention I am trying to justify further, that *subjectivity* should be taken as a central concept for the scientific discipline of human psychology. In contrast to the neighbouring disciplines—sociology, social anthropology and ethnology[6]—in psychology the search for knowledge is mainly concerned with the individual. But not just the individual as a "collection" of diverse statistical samples. The individual should also be seen as a real subject, as (1) possessing conscious experiences (perspectives, feelings, beliefs, desires, judgements, decisions, responsibilities and so on), (2) having agency, acting towards another entity—the object and (3) constituting specific subjective truths of the external world (material, discursive and symbolic). One could ask how this approach differs from psychological phenomenology (e.g. Jonathan Smith's Interpretative Phenomenological Analysis). My answer at this moment is that it doesn't in principle—psychologically it aims similarly deep and is similar in sensitivity towards diversity, but is nonetheless very specific and more complex. And, as phenomenology deals with well-defined paradigms and theories, I prefer the broader concept of subjectivity. We will see that there are plenty of good reasons for turning our attention to subjectivity, not least that psychology would benefit from this ontological appeal.

[6] In addition to the merits to be brought to the journal *Subjectivity* for opening up a space for an interdisciplinary discussion on subjectivity, the vast amount of knowledge on subjectivity recently accumulated in ethnology should be appreciated. A remarkable series of monographs has been published under the editorship of Tanya Luhrmann and Steven Parish since the start of the third millennium (15 volumes of *Ethnographic Studies in Subjectivity* by 2022). The 2007 volume, *Subjectivity: Ethnographic Investigations,* edited by Joao Biel, Byron Good and Arthur Kleinman offers a systematic and convincing conceptualization of the social-anthropological substantiation of subjectivity (focusing on the integration of "affect, cognition, moral responsibility, and action" (Biel et al., 2007b, p. 1)), despite being born out of frustration at the neglect of the subject in medicine. In their essay, Kleinman and Fitz-Henry highlight the importance of history, cultural specificity, political allocation and economic position in determining human subjectivity in contrast to biological determination: "Our subjectivities certainly have a biology, but they also, and perhaps more critically, have an equally influential history, cultural specificity, political location, and economic position" (Kleinman & Fitz-Henry, 2007, pp. 53). These aspects in particular are the source of heterogeneities, conflicts and contingencies of moral engagement that result in the uncontrollability and ignorance that define our human qualities (Kleinman & Fitz-Henry, 2007, pp. 52–65).

1.3   FROM POSITIVISM TO CRITICAL PSYCHOLOGY AND BEYOND

This part is best introduced by reference to the pioneering work of Paul Feyerabend (1975/2010), who, under the flag of "scientific anarchism," pointed out the manipulative nature of contemporary science, which is admired enthusiastically in mainstream psychology.

> Science education as we know it today has precisely this aim. It simplifies 'science' by simplifying its participants: first, a domain of research is defined. The domain is separated from the rest of history... and given a 'logic' of its own. A thorough training in such a 'logic' then conditions those working in the domain; it makes *their actions* more uniform and it freezes large parts of the *historical process* as well. Stable 'facts' arise and persevere despite the vicissitudes of history. An essential part of the training that makes such facts appear consists in the attempt to inhibit intuitions that might lead to blurring of boundaries. A person's religion, for example, or his metaphysics, or his sense of humour (his *natural* sense of humour and not the inbred and always rather nasty kind of jocularity one finds in specialized professions) must not have the slightest connection with the scientific activity. His imagination is restrained, and even his language ceases to be his own. This is again reflected in the nature of scientific 'facts' which are experienced as being independent of opinion, belief, and cultural background. (Feyerabend, ibid., p. 3)

The whole narrative of the historical emergence (in psychology) of a genuine focus on authentic subjectivity is relatively simple, much more simple than plots of Shakespeare's plays and Verdi's operas. Early psychology of the nineteenth and twentieth centuries, encouraged by flourishing natural sciences, acquired the positivist approach, thus claiming to be able of an objective, unbiased, value-neutral study of humans. As William J. Baker puts it:

> Subjects had to be treated as objects rather than as persons, so as to minimize or, if possible, eliminate any serious role for *their* individual predilections as well. Individual differences could only be seen as deviations from the much-sought-after general (and, preferably, deterministic) "laws" for our science. This naturally gravitated to a description of psychological phenomena in terms of variables rather than in terms of people because this allowed for a seemingly objective language that did not entail any responsibility for individual subjects. It was uncritically and almost universally

accepted that variables were the *same* variables for all subjects. (Baker, 1992, p. 10)

As psychology evolved in the 20th century, its practitioners manifested an almost neurotic need to be seen as scientific... this led them to reject the subjective world (i.e., the person) precisely because this was not in the physical domain. (Baker, 1992, p. 13)

The critique of the early and positivist psychology is, however, also openly political:

It was, of course, the "exigencies of business enterprise" that demanded a view of the worker as a nonthinking, nonfeeling machine that could be selected and trained solely according to the interests of the employer. The same exigencies urged the definition of psychology's mission as "prediction and control," with engineering efficiency, which included the understanding of psychological subject matter in terms of independent and dependent variables. (Tolman, 1991, p. 4)

Even the mechanistic stimulus-response behaviorism of Watson was relevant to somebody's interests, namely those of capital and its managers. This, the Critical Psychologists maintain, proves to be the case for all of Western psychology's nomothetic psychology. A psychology that deals with averages in the hopes of achieving generality through abstraction can never become relevant to the particular individual. But this is precisely what happens with our insistence on the measurement and statistical treatment of independent and dependent variables. This is altogether more suited to capital's need to manipulate the masses than to shedding light on the experience or problems of individuals. (Tolman, 1991, p. 5)

The "fear" of subjectivity concerned not only the object of study in psychology, but also the researcher, who was expected to be neutral and value-free:

if that holds for our subjects, why does it not hold for our experimenters? Why does it not hold for their interpretations of what they observe? (Baker, 1992, p. 11)

From this perspective, positivist psychology provided knowledge which secured both epistemological and political power in creating psychological knowledge. A *certain* power that became subject of massive critique years later. After decades of development of positivist sociology and psychology, Max Horkheimer, within the early Frankfurt school, formulated his "manifesto" *Traditional and critical theory* (1937). It took, however, another 30 years, until this critique from the left found a comprehensive platform in psychology—in the Critical Psychology of the late 1960s in Germany, initiated and led primarily by Klaus Holzkamp in West-Berlin from a Marxist position. Holzkamp rephrases his argumentation of that time for the necessity to create critical psychology in 1991. The accent on subjectivity, delightfully, was central in this revolutionary critique:

> Thus, generally speaking, the development of human subjectivity, as the possibility of conscious control over one's own life conditions, always and necessarily requires moving beyond individuality toward participation in the collective determination of the societal process: If the individual life conditions are the individually relevant societal life conditions, then the individual, taken as a solitary being, does not have the power consciously to determine them, but rather remains necessarily at the mercy of the circumstances of existence and can only react to present contingencies instead of providing for his or her own existence in a human manner. To the extent that the individual life circumstances are in fact relevant and that their societal interconnectedness and determinedness increase, the single individual can determine his or her own life circumstances and thus become an individual subject, but only in union with others as a moment of a social subject. (Holzkamp, 1991, pp. 58–59)

> it is no wonder that in recent times distinct alternative conceptions of psychology that introduce subjectivity, everyday life, and spontaneity as objects of psychological investigation have emerged and become widespread… What remains unclear, however, is how the inclusion of subjectivity in psychology as advocated by these conceptions squares with the demand for scientific objectivity. Does the assumption remain that subjectivity and objectivity are exclusive of one another, and is one thereby forced to reject or limit psychology's claim that it is scientific for the sake of subjectivity? Or is it possible in psychology to develop a concept of scientific objectivity that does not require the elimination of subjective self-experience?… It is therefore still necessary to consider subjectivity as a problem of psychological method. (Holzkamp, 1991, p. 66)

And then, in a "second wave" since the 1990s, scholars in the UK and elsewhere took over in developing critical psychology towards a well justified set of respected approaches to the human subject. This meant developing further the original argumentation line against bourgeois nature of the "experimental and variable based" simplifying psychologies, accused of the purpose to manipulate/exploit people.

> The implications for a critique of psychology can be summarized as follows: In its predominant objectivistic direction, psychology has misapprehended the activity and subjectivity of concrete human beings living in historically determined societal conditions as the behavior or experience of abstract individuals standing opposed to and determined by an environment (which itself is misunderstood in naturalistic and ahistorical terms). This misjudgement was not just a theoretical inadequacy stemming from the implicit adoption of an erroneous epistemological postulate of immediacy that need simply be given up. Rather, just like its subjectivistic inversion, which hypostatizes individuals as ultimate empirical units of analysis whose forms of living are explained by indwelling essential powers, it is an expression of "necessarily false consciousness." This consciousness, which arises spontaneously from the all-embracing forms of motion of the capitalist mode of production and which reifies them, reflects the actual inverted relations on the surface of bourgeois society: the privateness of individuals isolated from one another, whose societal relations appear in the form of natural relations among things. (Maiers, 1991, p. 29)

Along with political addressing of the "devil" of bourgeois interest of the mainstream psychology which ignored the human subjectivity as a plausible ontological substance, there was, however, in parallel, an epistemic movement building on the linguistic turn (Wittgenstein) since the 1920s, exploiting later constructivist principles (Berger & Luckmann, 1966) and developing into discursive psychology (cf. Curt 1994; Parker 2002).

> because discourse is the primary arena for human action, understanding and intersubjectivity. (Potter, 2003, p. 2)

> discourse is the fundamental medium for human action. Rather than seeing its fundamental analytic aim as being to attempt to open up the mythic black box where psychology has been thought to be hiding since Descartes and Locke developed their arguments, it is focused on the public realm which people have access to when they are dealing with other people. Its basic methodological and analytic principles follow from its meta-theoretical, theoretical and conceptual arguments, although these are further supported through the empirical fruitfulness in particular studies. (Potter, 2003, pp. 4–5)

This language-based psychology served as a synergetic amplifier for the original Critical Psychology in highlighting our subjectivity. So, the concept of subjectivity (in psychology) has a double justification: the political and the epistemic. Psychology ignoring the subjectivity of humans would be manipulative and poor.

1.4 Towards the Integration of Psychology

Reviewing the psychological "scripture" on subjectivity also leads us to conclude that psychology, after over a hundred years of institutionalized development as a scientific discipline, suffers from *fragmentation* on several levels. And fragmentation is also behind the neglect of such a complex concept as subjectivity. Several scholars note the fragmentation of psychology when pointing to failures either in the identity of psychology (Elms, 1975), its philosophical roots and development (Brown & Stenner, 2009), or the role of theory in psychology (Rey, 2017). It is well expressed in the words of Danzinger:

> The story of twentieth-century academic psychology is the story of an ultimately unsuccessful struggle against an even more obvious fragmentation... Psychologists had gained an academic foothold by doing experiments on such topics as sensation, perception and memory. For some time, that remained the respectable core of the discipline, but how test intelligence related to this core was far from clear. It was much easier to annex such a field institutionally than to assimilate it intellectually. (Danzinger, 1997, p. 85)

The deformed branches and schools of psychology, each of them strongly supported by particular theories, academic institutions and psychology departments, evolved throughout the twentieth century until the crisis of psychological knowledge in the 1970s (cf. Parker, 1989). As Elms observed in 1975 from the Mecca of modernist (social) psychology—the western shore of the Atlantic:

> During the past decade, ... many social psychologists appear to have lost not only their enthusiasm but also their sense of direction and their faith in the discipline's future. Whether they are experiencing an identity crisis, a paradigmatic crisis, or a crisis of confidence, most seem agreed that a crisis is at

hand.[7] ... Indeed, confidence has ebbed so dramatically that some critics within social psychology (e.g. Gergen, 1973) have returned to questioning whether the field is really a science – a question that critics outside the field have never abandoned. (Elms, 1975, pp. 967–968)

Similarly, Stam et al. (1998, p. 153) are sceptical of the contribution social psychology makes to psychological knowledge about the individual:

The individualism of social psychology characterizes individuals who do not exist but come into being only at the conclusion of a complicated set of methodological practices; practices that extract bits of "data" from individual "subjects" in such a way as to obliterate the identity and experience of any *one* of those "subjects" as persons.

Rey (2017) is critical of how psychological theory is tackled. "Theory, as such, has been mistreated in psychology due to its subordination to empirical facts or to its use as a dogma. In both cases, theory is reduced to labels or definitions used a priori, which are imposed on the information coming from the studied phenomenon, instead of being used as a general system of intelligibility [in an epistemological sense], from which new meaning can be produced during professional and research practices." Rey's "hidden" positivist position, with its markedly deductive expectation concerning theory per se, should be complemented with an inductive position, highlighting the need for bottom-up theories—e.g. grounded theory (Strauss & Corbin, 1994). However, bottom-up theories, despite the range and popularity of studies devoted to them, tend to deal with narrow issues in psychology and have yet to contribute a major psychological theory. In this messy theoretical constellation of psychology, Rey (2017) sees subjectivity

as a culturally, socially and historically located human production, characterized by units of symbolical processes and emotions, which appear together

---

[7] Elms (1975) expands on other social science disciplines as well: "These widespread self-doubts about goals, methods, and accomplishments are by no means unique to social psychology. Similar doubts have been expressed recently within many other areas of psychology, particularly the closely related fields of personality research (Carlson, 1971; Fiske, 1974), developmental psychology (Wohlwill, 1973), and clinical psychology (Albee, 1970; Farberow, 1973). Serious self-questioning has developed simultaneously in the other social sciences, including sociology (Gouldner, 1970), anthropology (Hymes, 1972), and economics (Roberts, 1974)" (Elms, 1975, p. 968).

as subjective singular configurations, both of which configure social and individual subjectivities in their complex interweavings. In contraposition to the individualistic psychology that had prevailed during the first half of the XX century, in the 1960s there was a turn towards a social psychology focused on socially engendered psychological phenomena. Since the 1980s, the most innovative and critical trends within psychology have been based on terms like discourse, deconstruction, relations of power, gender and so on, omitting the different paths of subjectivation, through which those processes are subjectively produced by individuals and social groups. This gap does not imply rejecting those important concepts, but implies complementing them by facing the complex challenges that come with the study of human phenomena. Subjectivity ... is an alternative to fill this gap. (Rey, 2017)

From a cultural-historical standpoint there is a justified desire, or rather, challenges that need to be tackled before a theory of subjectivity can be advanced (Rey, 2017).

1. To advance a new ontological definition of what subjectivity is, making explicit the differences with other concepts that have characterized psychology, which have kept it restricted to individual phenomena. Subjectivity integrates processes and configurations, which are engendered within cultural-social life, but which, at the same time, do not reproduce cultural social life. Being generated within culture, subjectivity does not depart from any universal structured principle. Subjectivity is emancipated from psyche as a natural system and, at the same time, is a resource for emancipation from the socially dominant institutionalized order.

2. The need to integrate a qualitative side of human phenomena, both social and individual, understanding each of these configured within the other through specific subjective senses resulting from the subjective configuration of the other. Despite one being configured within the other, social and individual subjectivities represent two different sites of subjective productions, maintaining tensional and contradictory relations between them.

3. An attempt to define integrative and dynamic concepts capable of advancing an understanding of how the systems of socio-cultural historical experiences and realities are configured into new kinds of subjective phenomena, whose generative character is the basis for the co-developed system of culture-subjectivity.

Subjectivity, from a cultural-historical standpoint, has an integrative function regarding the taxonomy of concepts traditionally used by psychology. At the same time, the definition of subjectivity proposed here permits an understanding of the individual subjective processes as part of cultural social realities, both of which are reciprocally configured. (Rey, 2017)

Thus, in highlighting the need for an integral psychological basis, Brown and Stenner (2009) introduce the term "second-order psychology":

We propose something like a kind of "second-order psychology" which attempts to pursue the psychological across the complex cultural and material forms that it takes. If "first-order psychology" is the attempt to replicate and reproduce the psychological under narrow, laboratory-like conditions with the ambition of putting the mechanisms of human action "under the microscope", so to speak, then "second-order psychology" is all about following human experience through the myriad of forms that it takes, including the forms mediated by scientific psychology itself. ... we should take guidance from those commentators and experts on experience who seem to be most relevant – ...it may be literature, ...molecular biology, ...sociology, at other times art. (Brown & Stenner, 2009, p. 5)

There are various reasons why Brown and Stenner felt the necessity to define and elaborate on this concept. Most of them are historical— (first-order) psychology suffers from the childhood trauma of being born in the period of positivist enthusiasm and was thus deprived of its initial happy playful years of self-seeking only to be confronted instead with (self-imposed) expectations of high performance from the very onset. Then there are the high institutional demands of the employment institutions in the modernist era dominated by pragmatist values and the military, personnel and machinery needs of the First World War. Brown and Stenner (2009, p. 202) provide a developmental psychology diagnosis: "psychology has grown old before its time, but without the maturity and wisdom that should accompany the ageing process."

1.5   FROM SELF, VIA "THE PERSON," TO PSYCHOLOGICAL SUBJECTIVITY AND THE ART-OF-LIVING

Let us start by looking at the historical state of mind in the early twentieth century, when institutionalized psychology was about the pursuit of positivist goals and an obsession with the particularization of the human psyche in an effort to ensure it met the requirements of a true "science." However, at that time, strong integrative psychological thinking existed in parallel—but outside of psychology. For example, in 1919 the German/ Swiss psychiatrist and philosopher Karl Jaspers published his *Psychology of Worldviews* (*Psychologie der Weltanschauungen*, Jaspers, 1919), at the peak of his psychiatric and psychological period. In it he distinguished between worldview teaching and psychology of worldview. In worldview teaching the main categories are the subject and the object, the soul(s) and the world; and the relationship between them is explored specific to each worldview. In psychology, there are no solid categories available, just (various types of) attitude. For those interested in worldview (worldview being a complex psychological category far from the particularized variables of "scientific psychology") there are three types of attitude: owing to the subject–object dualism there are *attitudes towards objects* (which may be active, contemplative or mystic) and *self-reflexive attitudes* (which may be contemplative, or active—active in the sense of enjoyment, asceticism and self-design), while the third type of attitude is superordinated to the previous types of attitude—Jaspers calls them *enthusiastic attitudes* (in contemporary social sciences and humanities jargon these would be agency, dynamic or pro-active attitudes). As we will proceed through the various substantiations of human subjectivity (Foucault, Curt, Brown and Stenner), we will find links to all three types of attitude (and their different forms) defined by Jaspers, as they constitute what I would call modes of becoming a subject (marking out the existentialist pathway he would follow in the next decades).

To consider the nature of psychological subjectivity it is helpful to draw on Foucault's philosophical and sociological definition of the self. Foucault focused his attention to the subject in later years, following the decades he spent studying knowledge and power. On the question of what the subject (the self) is and whether it is a substance Foucault states:

> It is not a substance. It is a form, and this form is not primarily or always identical to itself. You do not have the same sort of relationship to yourself

when you constitute yourself as a political subject who goes to vote or speaks at a meeting and when you are seeking to fulfil your desires in a sexual relationship. Undoubtedly there are relationships and interferences between these different forms of subject; but we are not dealing with the same type of subject. In each case, one plays, one establishes a different type of relationship to oneself. (Foucault, 1998, p. 290)

With the advent of the twenty-first century, the need to actively take human subjectivity into account is re-emerging in psychology. Now not only as a critique of mainstream psychology, but with a much bolder aim. The importance of subjectivity for/in psychology is highlighted by Rey (2017):

Subjectivity … does not represent just another concept of psychology, but a new ontological definition of human phenomena. Subjectivity emerges as a new qualitative human phenomenon defined as the unit between symbolical processes and emotions... (N)one of the (previous) psychological theories that refer directly or indirectly to subjectivity formulate a theory based on such a complex system.

Therefore, in spite of Foucault's rejection of a substance-seeking view of the subject, any effort to capture the "substance" that would lead us to the ontology of subjectivity is more than welcome. This frustration was still well captured by Blackman et al. in 2008: "What we are dealing with here … is an apparent inability to develop a complex and distinctive ontology that takes the subject as its central and foremost focus rather than explaining it in terms of a variety of other ontological principles" (Blackman et al., 2008, p. 8). Gergen (1998), e.g. speaks about "the person" and focuses on its textual definition. He seeks to highlight the diversity of textual representations of one and the same person—in culture, scientific discourse and in the laboratory.

The psychological subject is pre-eminently a textual being, born of a confluence of discursive practices. In generating the sense of a subject to be elucidated, the investigator can scarcely escape tradition; to do so would be the fail in achieving intelligibility. Yet, molding character from the available repositories of discourse is a precarious undertaking. Accounts of character – what it is to be a coherent and identifiable person – are first of all possessions of the populace. (Gergen, 1998, p. 111)

A genuine psychological understanding of the person, as sought by Gergen, requires us to integrate the cultural context (persons can only become intelligible if the cultural contexts of their existence are taken into account), the prevailing scientific theoretical paradigms (including competing ones) and evidence provided by data/methodology/computation/analysis "games." Moreover, it is not only the object of the study—the "person"—who is subject to these diverse aspects of representation (and interpretation!), but also the psychologist. Thus, the knowledge on the "person in focus of the study" is the result of "multiple-coding" in texts/discourses.

Or, as Arribas-Ayllon and Walkerdine (2008) put it: "The subject is not so much a 'thing' but a *position* maintained within relations of force – the mother, the wife, the father, the worker, the child. The delinquent, the patient, the criminal, and so forth. Furthermore, these multiple positionings are contradictory and discontinuous; they are not roles that pre-existing subjects take up, but an emergent space formed among vestors of force-relations" (ibid, p. 94).

In setting the stage for psychological subjectivity it may also be useful to explore a side alley called "where is the psychological located?" As Brown and Stenner (2009) state, "the psychological" may be "inside"—for cognitivists and phenomenologists relying on Cartesian and Kantian tradition, or "outside"—for strict behaviourists and discursive psychologists relying on pragmatism, speech philosophy and Wittgenstein, and, lastly, both (inside and outside)—"the psychological is not thinkable without linguistic mediation, and yet neither is it reducible to language" (Brown & Stenner, 2009, p. 7). However, they question whether the expectation that a solid definition of the (psychological) subject as such can be achieved is realistic:

> The subject [the psychological subject!] has always been the central puzzle of psychology – how is it that the biological, the social and the psychic come together in human thought, feeling and action? However, as work in critical psychology has demonstrated at length, the work of sewing together body, mind and society need not be approached with the reference to a bounded subject as such. (Brown & Stenner, 2009, pp. 175–176)

This fuzzy approach to subjectivity draws attention to contextual aspects. The external contexts of the subject may relate to history and culture (e.g. Gergen), power (e.g. Foucault), language and discourse (e.g.

Potter) or the dynamics of the unconscious (e.g. Lacan). Similarly, Curt, back in 1994, pointed to the necessity of integrating the "inner" subject and the "outer" contexts of power/institutions/ideology/things. Curt also notes what is "in between"—the discourses and their tectonics as seemingly autonomous entities. So, we can sum up this topological reflection on psychological subjectivity by stating that we need to search for the psychological both inside and outside (the subject), and in between.

Let's look again at the relationship between subjectivity and the discipline of psychology. The definition of subjectivity has, according to Rey (2017), the following theoretical implications:

1. Psychical functions, once they are subjectively configured, become self-generative subjective productions. This means that intellectual, motor, or any other operation become sources of subjective senses, transforming psychological functions into motives for their own functioning. Motivation becomes intrinsic to the psychical function itself. Personality, or any other concept used to refer to an individual subjective system, is configured in action, instead of being an a priori determinant of the action. In any case, subjective configurations of personality are responsible for a certain congruency that it is possible to perceive in individual trajectories. Subjectivity as a system is engaged in actions through the subjective configurations of those actions.

2. The definition of psychological functions and actions as subjectively configured processes allows the transcendence of psychological classification based on behavioral/symptomatic entities. This stresses the understanding of behaviors and psychological "pathological entities", such as those formulated via DSM III, IV, V and other classifications, as subjectively configured processes. This comprehension breaks down any standardization of individuals or groups as carriers of those labels. The study of subjective configurations is always a singular process.

3. Individual and social actions are simultaneously configured in individuals and in social scenarios within which individual actions take place, and are in tension with one another. The subjective system is not the actor of its own configurations; the actors are the individuals and social agents that actively and reflexively create their own paths, taking their own decisions during their experiences. The relevance of the concept of subject is stressed by Frosh as follows: "human subjects may be 'socially constructed', but from that constructed position *they exert choices which*

are never quite reducible to the forces that constructed them[8] in the first place." (Frosh, 2002, p. 3)

Rey's detailed argument on the importance of subjectivity in human agency can be amplified by Foucault's considerations of the self. The self was Foucault's third (and unfinished) area of thought, after knowledge and power. In his thinking on the self, Foucault actually advances against the discursive foundations of his structuralist/poststructuralist thought on knowledge and power. Foucault highlights the "active role of the self, reflecting on itself and thereby producing the subject" (Alvesson & Skölberg, 2000, p. 230). Thus in an "anti-Gergen" sense Foucault rejects the "postmodern view on subjectivation as a result of a 'free play' with signs" (in texts) (Alvesson & Skölberg, ibid., p. 148). In other words, the subject is "not primarily a social construction, but a construction of the self reflecting on the self" (ibid, p. 230). Foucault introduces the instruments/operations that enable the becoming of a subject. He calls these the "technologies of self":[9]

[technologies of self] enable the individuals to perform by themselves or with the help of others certain operations on their bodies and souls, minds, acts and ways of being in order to change themselves in a way reaching to certain state of happiness, purity, wisdom, perfection or immortality. (Foucault, 1988/2000, p. 188)

Foucault also defends subjectivity/self (inherently diversified) against the Western obsession with the (singular) truth:

And it is precisely the historical constitution these various forms of the subject in relation to the games of truth which interest me. (Foucault, 1998, p. 291)

After all, why truth? Why are we concerned with truth, and more so than with care of the self? And why must the care of the self occur only through the concern for truth? I think we are touching on a fundamental question here, what I would call the question for the West: How did it come about

---

[8] My emphasis.

[9] There are four kinds of technologies, according to Foucault (1988/2000): (1) production technologies, (2) technologies of signs, meanings and symbols, (3) technologies of power determining agency of individuals, leading to subordination to certain goals and control by others, and resulting in the objectification of the subject, and (4) technologies of the self-enabling individual agency.

that all the Western culture began to revolve around this obligation of truth
which has taken a lot of different forms. (Foucault, 1998, p. 295)

My aim here is not to follow the societal, cultural and political pathways
that could illustrate Foucault's accentuation of the truth-driving forces
manifested in the development of the self. I wish only to learn from it in
support of my presentation of the diverse forms of human subjectivity—
mainly cultural, value-based subjectivities. Is the complexity and unity of
plural subjectivities not a better substitute for the compulsive search for
(single universal) truth about us?

At this point I dare to say that the make-up of subjectivity (or constitution of the subject) can be considered a key, constitutive element of the
abovementioned "second-order psychology" proposed by Brown and
Stenner (2009). The central idea in "second-order psychology" is that
people must reflexively (in response to the world we live in or wish to live
in) create their own foundations—permanently and continuously. The relevant necessary contexts of our creative and reflexive foundationalism are
emotional, social, organic, cultural, material and the symbolic environment. As Brown and Stenner state:

> Whether one has consciously realised it or not, to live, to act, to think and
> to talk one must constantly negotiate a position between the impossible
> extremes of unrepeatable chaos and redundant order. (Brown & Stenner,
> 2009, p. 199)

In exploring the object of "second-order psychology," Brown and
Stenner (2009) go even beyond the concept of subjectivity. In searching
for a higher generalized level of knowledge/entity, above that of the
individual subject, this leads them to the concept of life—"or more precisely, of understanding how particular lives are extracted from the
*modes of existence, relations, normativities and processes which comprise
life-in-itself*" (Brown & Stenner, 2009, p. 176). Brown and Stenner
draw here on the work of British philosopher and psychologist Alfred
North Whitehead, for whom "the art of life ... concerns the active modification of one's environment, and the more sophisticated the organ-
ism, the more actively it transforms its surroundings. When it comes to
us human beings, this transformation and creation of the environment
becomes the most prominent fact in our existence" (Brown & Stenner,
2009, p. 201). Life can be elaborated as the "art of living": "Aim and
value are inescapable aspects of psychology once being is constructed in

relation to becoming, and ethics becomes a very real project of the coordination and harmonization of personal and collective existence" (Brown & Stenner, 2009, p. 201).

1.6 Diversity in Subjectivity

Another point about subjectivity is its *diversity*. In my academic work I tried (sometimes unconsciously at first) to approach subjectivity in a number of diverse contexts. Potential contexts were cultural, as well as environmental and political (e.g. within the study of human values), or physical/bodily, and at the same time evolutionary, but also socially normative, discursive and political (e.g. in the study of human sexuality and intimacy). Thus we can distinguish between a multilevel structure of possible *"units" of analysis for diverse subjectivities*—individual, cultural, collective—and *diverse topic-related subjectivities*—intimate, sexual, value-related, environmental, gender and political. The intersections of these categories roughly represent the research areas in which (my) scientific efforts and contributions can be located.

Thus, I dare to assume that the research on cultural, sexual and societal/community subjectivity concerning human values, sexuality and intimacy presented in the following chapters illustrates this and can be integrated into the "second-order psychology" proposed by Brown and Stenner (2009). I somewhat boldly suggest that the figurative diversity of subjectivity, presented in Chaps. 2, 3 and 4 is actually a substantiation of the various possible reflexive foundations of the psychological. Such an approach materializes what Brown and Stenner call "the project of reflexive foundationalism around psychology – continuously reinventing what the psychological can be in the course of following its complex patterns of mediation" (Brown & Stenner, 2009, p. 176).

1.7 Social Representations

The epistemological theory known as *social representations* was developed at the end of the 1960s by Serge Moscovici. He was interested in how new scientific concepts enter public discourse and how they become active players in people's everyday lives; how scientific knowledge becomes common sense. Here I agree with Denise Jodelet (2008), who, reflecting on almost 30 years of enthusiastic use of Moscovici's theory, and referring to his pioneering work (1961),[10] claims that "one of the most serious gaps in developing Moscovici's heuristic proposals refers to the processes of production of social representations, namely anchoring and objectification. They are referred to by many researchers but rarely with a complete account. Very few take into account the different phases identified by Moscovici" (Jodelet, 2008, p. 425). But my goal in this book is not to analyse the theory of social representations. Rather, encouraged by Jodelet's critique, I consider two processes that are crucial for the production of social representations, anchoring and objectification. Both seem optimal for identifying/extracting psychological subjectivity from diverse research endeavours.

If we are to draw attention to new perspectives on psychological phenomena and highlight the diversity of human subjectivity, subjectivity needs to be anchored into familiar concepts and patterns. I have presented the history and current views on psychological subjectivity (in this chapter) to provide a suitable anchoring environment. The more important of the two processes for me is the process whereby "new phenomena" are objectified. Hence we need to find specific, concrete, tangible forms of the phenomenon in focus—human subjectivity. We can call these *figurative forms*—as they represent the visualized, seizable forms of subjectivity that can be manipulated. Each of the new forms (or categories) of human psychological subjectivity that I will introduce can be perceived as figurations of the social representation of human psychological subjectivity. In this way I intend to exploit the theory of social representations as a "tray" on which to serve the figurative diversity of psychological subjectivity.

SUMMARY

In brief, subjectivity can be defined as

"culturally, socially and historically located human production, characterized by units of symbolical processes and emotions, which appear together as subjective singular configurations, both of which configure social and individual subjectivities in their complex interweavings… **Subjectivity** … does not represent just another concept of psychology, but **a new ontological definition of human phenomena**. Subjectivity emerges as a new qualitative human phenomenon defined as the unit between symbolical processes and emotions" (Rey, 2017). To identify subjectivity psychologically we need

---

[10]Moscovici, S. 1961. La Psychanalyse, Son Image et Son Public. Paris: Presses Universitaires de France.

to look inside and outside (the subject), and in between. Or, from a Jaspersian perspective, to understand the subject(s), we need to explore their attitudes towards objects, their self-reflexive attitudes and their enthusiastic attitudes (agency).

Moreover, subjectivity is:

- Plural;
- Self-generative/conditioned by self-reflection and technologies of the self; and
- Has to be "lived."

These key attributes are consistent with those given by Blackman et al. in their "manifesto" of subjectivity—the editorial to the first issue of the journal *Subjectivity* in 2008:

> subjectivity ...we could call experience of being subjected [**self-generative nature of subjectivity**]... subjectivity ... is the experience of the lived [!] multiplicity of positionings [**plural**]. (Blackman et al., 2008, p. 6)

I tried to show subjectivity could be treated as a central concept in the scientific discipline of human psychology. And if yes, then there is the question: What would be the implications? Are we facing a paradigmatic change in psychology? As Thomas Kuhn observed, the ruling paradigm inspires research up to the point where new findings fail to fit into it. From that point on, a new paradigm starts to operate and all existing knowledge is questioned to see if it fits into the new paradigm—usually it does not. I will try to consider these issues again in the final chapter. But for now, let us start by at least being cautious about the essentialist psychological truths and laws from the first century of psychology and their usefulness for coping with the main challenges of our civilization in the twenty-first century.

CHAPTER 2

Values, Individual and Cultural Subjectivity and Predictions of Political Participation (in Slovakia)

Abstract This chapter looks at values (as phenomena of cultural subjectivity) in terms of the rapid social change that began after the fall of the iron curtain in 1989. Empirical findings from countries which overcame several decades of communist totalitarian regimes in Eastern-Central Europe, in particular Slovakia, contribute to the development and refinement of Shalom Schwartz's structural theory of values. This chapter presents findings from a comprehensive study on the structure of human values that juxtaposes several Eastern European countries against several Western European countries, focusing particularly on certain aspects relating to Slovakia (Schwartz, S. H., Bardi, A., & Bianchi, G., Value adaptation to the imposition and collapse of communist regimes in East-Central Europe. In S. A. Renshon & J. Duckitt (Eds.), *Political psychology: Cultural and crosscultural foundations* (pp. 217–237). Macmillan Press Ltd, 2000). The hypotheses of this study were derived from the observation that adjusting to life under communism had clear value implications. The close supervision, strict rules and suppression of initiative, risk and innovation all undermined autonomy values and mastery values. The communist regimes may have unintentionally fostered the acquisition of conservativism values because disrupting the social order was dangerous. Moreover, the authoritarian nature of the regimes endorsed the hierarchical order and hierarchy values. The decline in mutual trust diminished egalitarian values—the voluntary commitment to the welfare of others. I also present

© The Author(s), under exclusive license to Springer Nature Switzerland AG 2022
G. Bianchi, *Figurations of Human Subjectivity*,
https://doi.org/10.1007/978-3-031-19189-3_2

the results of subsequent cross-cultural studies that build on Schwartz's theory of values and examine the links between basic human values, political values, ideology preferences, religiosity and civic activism—elements of the new civil society that was a work in progress in post-communist Europe—again with a special focus on Slovakia. These studies bring additional insights into cultural and political subjectivity.

2.1   Individual and Cultural Subjectivity "Encoded" in Values

At the beginning of the 1990s I had the privilege (along with my colleague Viera Rosová) of making Slovakia part of an international project on basic human values in a global context. The historical period after the Velvet Revolution was a great opportunity to study, under real-life conditions, the effects on society of 40 years of life under the totalitarian communist regimes in the former Soviet bloc—Central and Eastern European countries. The invitation came directly from Shalom Schwartz (The Hebrew University of Jerusalem).

The structural model of basic human values developed by Shalom Schwartz (1992)[1] builds on previous approaches to the conceptualization of human values (Rokeach, Hofstede).

The theory of values (Schwartz, 1992, 2012) is based on a conception of values containing six main features implicit in the writings of many theorists:

1. *Values are beliefs* linked inextricably to affect. When values are activated, they become infused with feeling. People for whom independence is an important value become aroused if their independence is threatened, despair when they are helpless to protect it, and are happy when they can enjoy it.

---

[1] Schwartz, S. H. (1992). Universals in the Content and Structure of Values: Theoretical Advances and Empirical Tests in 20 Countries. In M. P. Zanna (Ed.), *Advances in Experimental Social Psychology* (vol. 25, pp. 1–65). Academic Press. https://doi.org/10.1016/S0065-2601(08)60281-6

2. *Values refer to desirable goals* that motivate action People for whom social order, justice, and helpfulness are important values are motivated to pursue these goals.

3. *Values transcend specific actions and situations.* Obedience and honesty values, for example, may be relevant in the workplace or school, in business or politics, with friends or strangers. This feature distinguishes values from norms and attitudes that usually refer to specific actions, objects or situations.

4. *Values serve as standards or criteria.* Values guide the selection or evaluation of actions, policies, people, and events. People decide what is good or bad, justified or illegitimate, worth doing or avoiding, based on possible consequences for their cherished values. But the impact of values in everyday decisions is rarely conscious. Values enter awareness when the actions or judgments one is considering have conflicting implications for different values one cherishes.

5. *Values are ordered by importance relative to one another.* People's values form an ordered system of priorities that characterize them as individuals... This hierarchical feature also distinguishes values from norms and attitudes.

6. *The relative importance of multiple values guides action.* Any attitude or behavior typically has implications for more than one value. For example, attending church might express and promote tradition and conformity values at the expense of hedonism and stimulation values. The tradeoff among relevant, competing values guides attitudes and behaviors. Values influence action when they are relevant in the context (hence likely to be activated) and important to the actor. (Schwartz, 2012, pp. 3–4)

Basic values are beliefs about what is good or bad, what should and should not be done, what is desirable or undesirable, and enable the evaluation of everyday practices. The original ten types of individual values (represented by 57 single values) which the Schwartz Value Theory builds in are:

Self-Direction: independent thought and action—choosing, creating, exploring.
Stimulation: excitement, novelty and challenge in life.
Hedonism: pleasure or sensuous gratification for oneself.
Achievement: personal success through demonstrating competence in line with social standards.

Power: social status and prestige, control or dominance over people and resources.

Security: safety, harmony and stability of society, of relationships and of self.

Conformity: restraint of actions, inclinations and impulses likely to upset or harm others and violate social expectations or norms.

Tradition: respect, commitment and acceptance of the customs and ideas that one's culture or religion provides.

Benevolence: preserving and enhancing the welfare of those with whom one is in frequent personal contact (the "in-group").

Universalism: understanding, appreciation, tolerance and protection for the welfare of all people and nature.

These are organized into a system of *four higher-order values* forming two bipolar axes (Openness to Change, the opposite of Self-enhancement, and Conservation, the opposite of Self-transcendence). The structural nature of this model is expressed by its interpretative power: rather than ranking the subject on each of the 57 single values, it positions the subject in the plot structure (*individual-value subjectivity*) given by the two "axes" of the higher-order values being interpreted (see Fig. 2.1).

However, for the purposes of cross-cultural comparison, a theory of seven types of culture-level values was developed and empirically validated (Schwartz, 1992, 1994, 1999, 2012). The seven types are (again extracted from the original 57 single values): Conservatism, Intellectual Autonomy, Affective Autonomy, Hierarchy, Egalitarianism, Harmony and Mastery.

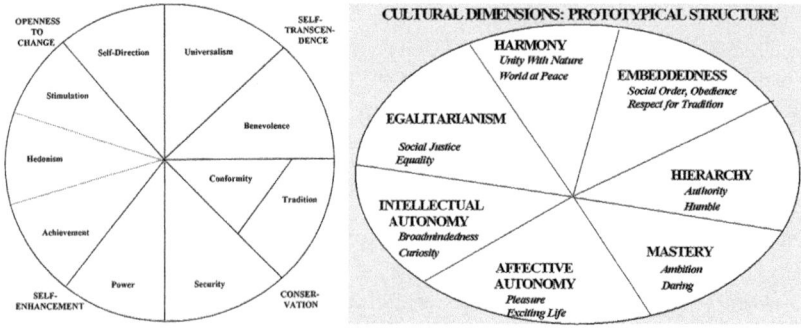

Fig. 2.1 Individual- and cultural-level structure of basic human values by Schwartz (from Schwartz, 1999)

The seven value-types create a structural plot, with mutually excluding/conflicting tendencies between the contrasting value types. Samples representing different cultures (here the units of analysis are cultural samples, each of them encompassing all the participants in one culture) can be positioned in this circular structure and then their proximity towards some of the cultural value types, as well as their relative distance from other cultures (*cultural value subjectivity*), can be quantified.

(A) *Structure of values in Slovakia in general*
   Let's look at a particular example. In a study by Schwartz, Bardi and Bianchi (2000)[2] hypotheses were derived from the observation that adaptation to life under communism has clear value implications. The close supervision, strict rules and the suppression of initiative, risk and innovation all undermine autonomy values and mastery values. Conversely, communist regimes may have encouraged the development of conservative values given that disrupting the communist order was dangerous. Moreover the authoritarian nature of the regime endorsed the hierarchical order and hierarchy values. The decline in mutual trust led to a decrease in egalitarian values—the voluntary commitment to pursing the welfare of others. The hypotheses of the study were that:

1. respondents in Eastern Europe would attribute greater importance to conservatism and hierarchy values, and
2. relatively low importance to intellectual autonomy, affective autonomy, egalitarianism and mastery values.

The aim of the comparative research was to contrast western countries—Denmark, Finland, France, West Germany, Greece, Italy, the Netherlands, Portugal, Spain, Sweden and Switzerland (Western Europe)—with eastern countries (post-communist countries)—Bulgaria, the Czech Republic, Estonia, Georgia, Hungary, Poland, Russia, Slovakia and Slovenia. The samples consisted of sets (of around 200 persons each) of Year 1–3 primary school teachers and university students. The empirical data (the Schwartz Value Survey

---

[2] Schwartz, S.H., Bardi, A. & Bianchi, G. (2000). Value Adaptation to the Imposition and Collapse of Communist Regimes in East-Central Europe. In: S. A. Renshon and J. Duckitt (Eds.), *Political Psychology: Cultural and Crosscultural Foundations* (pp. 217–237). Macmillan Press Ltd.

containing 57 items) was collected in 1992 and a repeat data collection was performed in 1997.

Both hypotheses were confirmed: there were significant differences between Western European and East-European countries (in both teachers and students): higher scores for conservatism and hierarchy values and lower scores for egalitarianism, and both forms of autonomy and mastery values in East-European countries. Moreover, no significant evidence was found for value change in East-European countries in 1992–1997.

In order to better understand the cultural subjectivity and situation in Slovakia, we can turn to the findings of Bunčák (2001) concerning the identity-forming effects of Christianity (the *conservative hierarchical* authority) on people. The effect of Christianity is amplified by (1) the way it ties in with Slovak national identity, (2) the fact the Christian community is the only identifiable one with historical roots in Slovakia, a predominantly rural country and (3) the indirect pressure to identify with the Christian faith exerted by the highly homogenous community.

(B) *Culture dominates over political ideology and nationality*

The plot of the location of individual national groups in the structure of second-order core values (Fig. 2.2) illustrates the strength of cultural determination in the direction of value preferences. For example, even after 40 years of communist regime in the German Democratic Republic, people in Eastern Germany express their value subjectivity closer to the West-Germans than to any other postcommunist country (Hungary, Slovakia, Czechia, Slovenia, Estonia, Romania or Poland). Similarly, French Canadians locate the closest to French, whereas English-speaking Canadians locate within the tight "English speaking" grouping—UK, New Zealand, Australia, Ireland. And Israelis are divided into Jewish and Arab —mutually distant groups—according to the second-order value structure.

(C) *Environmental values in Slovakia*

My "entry" into the field of human values came about as part of my involvement in environmental psychology. We were interested in how Slovakia performed on environmental values compared with over 30 international samples (Bianchi & Rosová, 1992). For this comparison we used three values from a pool of 57 values from the full list from the Schwartz Value Survey (SVS): *protecting the environment, preserving nature; unity with nature, fitting into nature; a world of beauty, in nature and the arts.* These three values constitute (along with some other val-

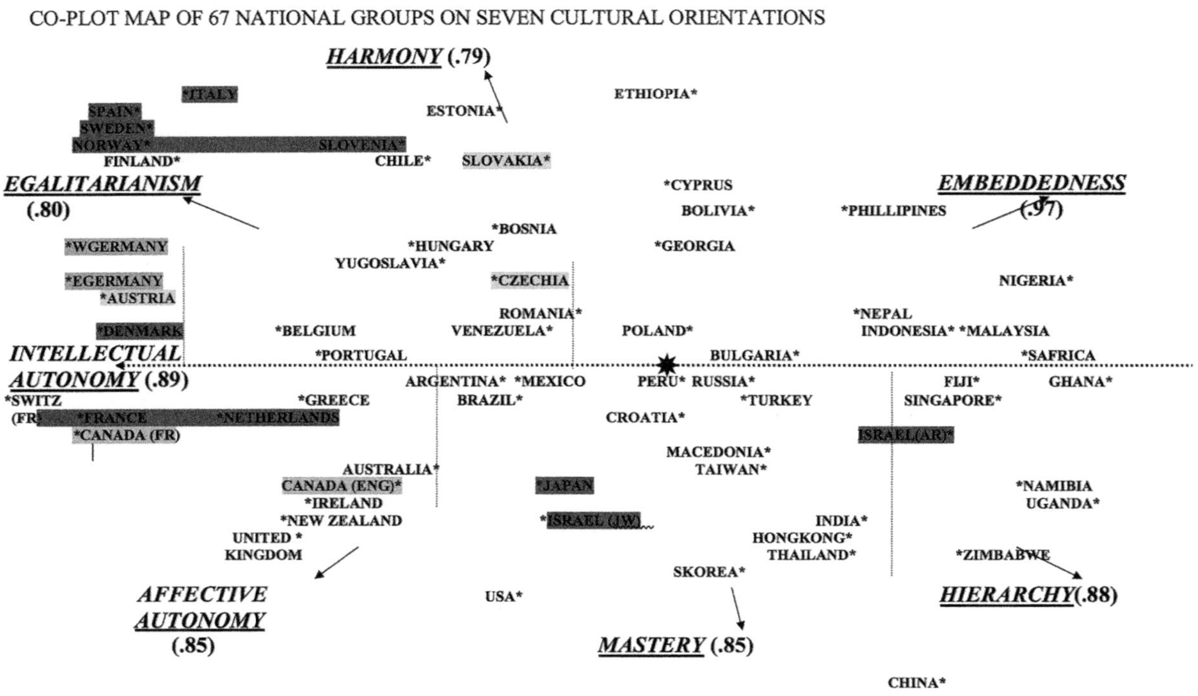

CO-PLOT MAP OF 67 NATIONAL GROUPS ON SEVEN CULTURAL ORIENTATIONS

Fig. 2.2 Position of cultural samples at the second-level (cultural) structure of basic personal values (adapted from Schwartz, 1999)

ues) the second-order value of HARMONY. Our sample consisted of elementary-school teachers and university students. The students from Slovakia ranked first of 30 international samples from Australia and Japan, Europe, Africa and the USA. By contrast the teachers from Slovakia ranked eighth, behind Italy, Mexico, Estonia-urban, Finland, Estonia-rural, Spain and Hungary. In the early 1990s the environment was, briefly after the fall of the iron curtain, a much more ambiguous topic for adults than it was for students. The best illustration of this generational difference in environmental values is data from East and West Germany. The East–West divide had no effect on student opinions as the environment was a highly referential value. However, among German teachers the East–West divide played an important role: West Germany teachers ranked 10th in Harmony, whereas East Germany teachers ranked 17th. One can assume that the cultural subjectivity, based on identification with a particular structure of basic personal values is enhanced by a specific *environmental subjectivity*.

Although these results showed analytical promise, I had to rather abruptly discontinue my research in this area in order to take up research in human sexuality (see Chap. 3). *Almost two decades later* I was again invited to participate in value-related research by the principal investigator, Prof. Shalom Schwartz. This time the focus was on political behaviour and entailed an international comparative study on the measurement and prediction of citizens' political involvement. The study led to several papers on the relationship between basic personal values and political values on the one hand and political decision-making, religiosity and political activism on the other. Slovakia was quite different to the general international picture. The cultural and political subjectivity can be illustrated as follows:

(D) *Differences in basic personal values play a decisive role in political thinking. But not in Slovakia.*
The main questions driving the study [3] were: *Do the political values held by the general public form a coherent system (that can be considered*

---

[3] Schwartz, S. H., Caprara, G. V., Vecchione, M., Bain, P., Bianchi, G., Caprara, M. G., Cieciuch, J., Kirmanoglu, H., Baslevent, C., Lonnqvist, J. E., Mamali, C., Manzi, J., Pavlopoulos, V., Posnova, T., Schoen, H., Silvester, J., Tabernero, C., Torres, C., Verkasalo, M., Vondrakova, E., Welzel, C., & Zaleski, Z. (2014). Basic Personal Values Underlie and Give Coherence to Political Values: A Cross National Study in 15 Countries. *Political Behavior, 36*(4), 899–930. https://doi.org/10.1007/s11109-013-9255-z

political subjectivity)? What is the source of this coherence? And *what differences are there between established Western non-communist democracies and post-communist countries given that basic values and political values take on different meanings?*
In the political domain political values express more basic personal values. As conceptualized by Schwartz, basic personal values (e.g. security, achievement, benevolence, hedonism) are organized along a circular continuum reflecting the conflicting, yet compatible, incentives of subjective motivations. The circular motivational structure (Fig. 2.1) lends coherence to political values. Empirical data from 16 countries on 5 continents (Europe, North America, South America, Asia and Oceania) were collected using 8 core political values and ten basic personal values from Schwartz. (see Frame 2.1).

Frame 2.1 Political Values

- Traditional morality: society should protect traditional religious, moral and family values.
- Blind patriotism: people should support and never criticize their country.
- Law and order: government should forbid disruptive activities and enforce obedience to the law.
- Free enterprise: government should not be involved in the economy.
- Equality: society should distribute opportunities and resources equally.
- Civil liberties: everyone should be free to act and think as they deem most appropriate.
- Foreign military intervention: nations should use military means to deal with international problems if necessary.
- Accepting immigrants: foreign immigrants contribute positively to our country.

The correlation and regression analyses supported almost all the hypotheses:
(*D.1*) *Basic values account for substantially more variance in political values than do age, gender, education and income.*

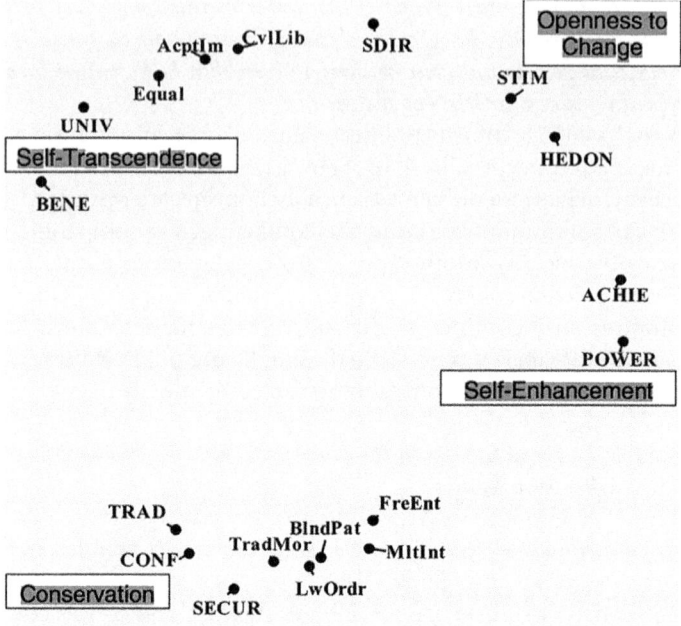

Fig. 2.3   Joint multidimensional scaling of ten basic personal values (at individual level) and eight political values (from Schwartz et al., 2014). Basic Values: ACHIE—achievement, HEDON—hedonism, STIM—stimulation, SDIR—self-direction, UNIV—universalism, BENE—benevolence, TRAD—tradition, CONF—conformity, SECU—security; Core Political Values: TradMor—traditional morality, LwOrdr—law and order, BlndPat—blind patriotism, MltInt—military intervention, FreEnt—free enterprise, CvlLib—civil liberties, AcptIm—accepting immigrants, Equal—equality (from Schwartz et al., 2014)

Multidimensional scaling analyses demonstrated, in graphical form, how the circular motivational structure of basic personal values organizes relations among core political values. This study supported the assumption that individual differences in basic personal values play a critical role in political thinking. In other words basic personal values create a solid basis for a specific individual value subjectivity, with a strong predictive effect on political subjectivity (Fig. 2.3).

(D.2) *Left–right ideology predicted voting in all countries except Ukraine and Slovakia.*

Further data[4] analysis was performed to determine if left–right (liberal–conservative) ideology contributed to voting behaviour and to what extent basic values account for ideological orientation. The results showed that left–right (liberal–conservative) ideology predicted voting in all countries except Ukraine. Basic values were good predictors of ideology (and thus voting) in most countries, especially in established democracies such as Australia, Finland, Italy, UK and Germany. The pattern of relations at the national/cultural level with the whole set of ten basic values revealed that the critical trade-off regarding ideology (left–right voting preferences) is between values relating to tolerance and protecting people's welfare (*universalism*) on the one hand and values relating to the preservation of the social order and status quo (*security*) on the other hand. A noteworthy exception was European post-communist countries, where basic personal values had little (Poland) or almost no (Ukraine, Slovakia) connection with ideology. Thus, in spite of the strong link between basic-value subjectivity (as individual-value subjectivity) and political-value subjectivity, values (cultural-level value subjectivity) were better predictors of ideology/political voting: the link is maintained when universalism-values dominate over security-values; conversely, when security-values dominate over universalism-values the link is weakened (e.g. as in Slovakia).

(*D.3*) *In Slovakia political orientation is strongly linked to religiosity: the more religious the person, the more right-wing and conservative they are.*
In the data analysis we also looked for relationships between religiosity and ideological political orientation (left–right, conservative-liberal).[5] The results showed that high religiosity is consistently

---

[4] Caprara, G. V., Vecchione, M., Schwartz, S. H., Schoen, H., Bain, P. G., Silvester, J., Cieciuch, J., Pavlopoulos, V., Bianchi, G., Kirmanoglu, H., Baslevent, C., Mamali, C., Manzi, J., Katayama, M., Posnova, T., Tabernero, C., Torres, C., Verkasalo, M., Lonnqvist, J. E., Vondrakova, E. & Caprara, M. G. (2017). Basic Values, Ideological Self-Placement, and Voting: A Cross-Cultural Study. *Cross-Cultural Research, 51*(4), 388–411. https://doi.org/10.1177/1069397117712194

[5] Caprara, G. V., Vecchione, M., Schwartz, S. H., Schoen, H., Bain, P. G., Silvester, J., Cieciuch, J., Pavlopoulos, V., Bianchi, G., Kirmanoglu, H., Baslevent, C., Mamali, C., Manzi, J., Katayama, M., Posnova, T., Tabernero, C., Torres, C., Verkasalo, M., Lonnqvist, J. E., Vondrakova, E. & Caprara, M. G. (2018). The Contribution of Religiosity to Ideology: Empirical Evidences from Five Continents. *Cross-Cultural Research, 52*(5), 524–541. https://doi.org/10.1177/1069397118774233

related to right-wing and conservative political preferences. We also found that this relationship held regardless of type of religion, or demographic parameter (sex, age, income, education). When the structure of basic values was taken into account, countries with a secular public sphere (Australia, Brazil, Chile, Germany, Finland, Israel, Japan, Ukraine, UK and USA) differed from countries where religiosity plays an important role in the public sphere (including Spain, Poland, Greece, Italy, Turkey and Slovakia). In the second set of (religious) countries, religiosity has an enormous effect on political orientation. This is not surprising, as religious subjectivity and value subjectivity are both instances of cultural subjectivity. But it does indicate that political subjectivity is amplified when there is high religious subjectivity.

(*D.4*) *Political activism can be predicted from people's value preferences—but less so in Slovakia compared to stable democracies.*

Another aspect that is interesting in terms of political psychology is political activism. The data mentioned above were also used to explore how political activism relates to citizens' value preferences (basic values). [6] Analyses have revealed key links between activism and values. Political activism is positively related to the values of self-transcendence and openness to change—when taking into account second-order individual basic values, mainly universalism and self-direction (autonomy of thought)—and when taking into account second-order cultural level basic values. On the other hand, political activism is negatively related to conservative values, particularly values constituting conformity and security (cultural-level basic values). Moreover, they interact as well: depending on the level of democratization in the country, there are differences in the strength of the relationship between individual/cultural basic values and political activism. This relationship was weakest in Slovakia and Poland and strongest in Finland. This analysis provides another viewpoint on value subjectivity and political subjectivity (activism is part of it), how they interconnect, and what they mean for people's lives.

[6] Vecchione, M., Schwartz, S. H., Caprara, G. V., Schoen, H., Cieciuch, J., Silvester, J., Bain, P., Bianchi, G., Kirmanoglu, H., Baslevent, C., Mamali, C., Manzi, J., Pavlopoulos, V., Posnova, T., Torres, C., Verkasalo, M., Lonnqvist, J. E., Vondrakova, E., Welzel, C. & Alessandri, G. (2015). Personal values and political activism: A cross-national study. *British Journal of Psychology, 106*(1), 84–106. https://doi.org/10.1111/bjop.12067

Summary

The aim of this chapter was to present diverse figurative examples of human subjectivity, based on basic human values, as well as political substance. It also offers some insights into the situation in Slovakia. The general psychological theory framing these is Schwartz's well-known theory of the structure of human values. The information obtained from the studies I participated in sheds new light on the societal and political reality in Slovakia, which is part of Western civilization in the third millennium and—at the same time—strongly shaped by its recent past. These figurative examples of human subjectivity contribute in a small way to the holistic efforts undertaken in the emergent second-order psychology.

CHAPTER 3

Sexual Subjectivity

Abstract This chapter is an overview of my exploration of sexual subjectivity. It begins with an attempt to define sexual subjectivity and then continues with a historical excursion into the era when interest in sexuality first began to emerge in modern medicine. Figuratively speaking, the subjectivity of scientific study of sexuality was born at that time. Besides signalling the beginning of a scientific approach to human sexuality, the encounter between sexuality per se and the medical environment (institutionalized medicine) introduced trauma into everyday sexuality in the Western world, a trauma from which we and the sexuality of the subject are still recovering today. Metaphorically I view the scientific medical interest in sexuality as having inflicted a sort of nosocomial trauma on sexuality. Here "nosocomial" refers to the institutionalized influence of medicine. The trauma was mainly the result of the institutionalized medical authorities backing the pathologizing of masturbation and homosexuality.

The chapter follows on from this with an epistemological discussion of the various discursive understandings of sexuality followed by an analysis of sexual performance—the phenomenological areas of sexual practice concerning the subjective meaning of sex and sexual satisfaction, and the motives and predictors of first sex. It closes with an analysis of cognitive strategies for coping with sexuality from the "forbidden zone" that were developed during the cognitive and cultural evolution and considers current social justifications of risky sexual practices. The contribution is then

G. Bianchi, *Figurations of Human Subjectivity*,
https://doi.org/10.1007/978-3-031-19189-3_3

enhanced by my thoughts on two studies that I led that dig deeply into issues such as the boundary between wanted and unwanted sex, as well as into the media dimensions of sex and violence, which lead into a reflection of the tensions between sexual intimacy and extimacy.

In the previous chapter I tried to explain that subjectivity is formulated and expressed in discourses materializing the whole range of possible values, norms, cultures, goals, criteria, figures and images; these are captured in words, texts and their tectonics, which each subject has to cope with. That is the background and context of sexual subjectivity. But the central question is: what is sexual subjectivity about? I propose that we accept that sexual subjectivity is understanding the sexual self—*our* sexual-selves and *others'* sexual-selves. And in the pages that follow I try to illustrate some of the figurative expressions of the substance of our sexual subjectivity, which I focused on in previous research—our perceptions of the meaning of sex (what does sex mean to us), sexual satisfaction, sexual motives, sexual taboos, risks and their justifications, as well as the distinction between wanted and unwanted sex and the roots of sexual violence.

In other words, we may ask: What does sex mean to people? What is the phenomenology of sex? And what does having (or not having) sex mean to people? What are their expectations? And what do they end up with? How does it feed into people's sexual and life satisfaction?

At this point one has to admit that there is a certain kind of *dualism in defining sexual subjectivity*. The first is the mainstream (psychology) approach, described above, aimed at the second-order psychology paradigm and is to be contrasted with the other approach—which draws on the critical sexuality-study paradigm. One of the first scholars to open this postmodern "pandora's box" of endless variability in sexuality was William Simon, who in 1996 wrote: "It may be something of an irony that human sexuality, frequently viewed as constant across the human record, is actually among the forms of behaviour most dependent upon contextualizing contingencies… Clearly, there are more reasons for being sexual than ways of being sexual" (Simon, 1996, pp. 115–116). The critical approach is applied to other sexuality contexts that are considered mandatory and relevant to sexual subjectivity. These include gender subjectivity, body subjectivity, intimate subjectivity and normative subjectivity. Fahs and McClelland (2016) put it thus: "what we currently know about sexuality leaves out a variety of different bodies, perspectives, identities, and stories, and that too often social and sexual scripts[1] are imposed upon people rather than learned from the ground up." The emphasis is primarily on "young women, ... adolescent sexuality and well-being, polyamory, female faking orgasm, sexting discourses, male sex work, sexual self-concept, and sexual entrepreneurship." The critical approach moves beyond individual interpretations of social reality to deeper recognition of how social norms, policies and relationships shape what people think about their sexual selves... [W]hat is often assumed the most private or the most "true" self—the sexual self—...[is] created and maintained in social, political and even national spaces... By using sexual subjectivities as a platform for putting forth a critical feminist analysis of sexuality, new and more complicated conceptualizations of sexual identities and sexual practices emerge[2] (Fahs & McClelland, 2016).

In the following chapter I will try to illustrate both our understanding of sexual subjectivity and try to indicate possible areas of overlap, as well as any tensions.

[1] On the Theory of Sexual Scripts see Sects. 3.2, 3.3, 4.2 and 5.4.
[2] The dualism of the mainstream approach and critical approach to sexual subjectivity reflects the essential distinction William Simon made in his *Postmodern Sexualities* (1996) in relation to the historical shifts in the epistemic-cultural paradigms of sexuality: modernization as naturalization and postmodernity as denaturalization. All the attempts to acquire and deepen knowledge about sexuality since the onset of sexology in the nineteenth century and through most of the twentieth century drew on material, natural and scientific arguments and justifications. We can perhaps see the removal of homosexuality as a mental disorder from the DSM in 1974 as the final symbolic act in the modernist approach or the breaking point in the postmodernist denaturalization of sexuality. "The denaturalized approach proposes that the sexual is socially constructed, that the origins of sexual desire can only be found in social life and its variable presence in the lives of specific individuals is predominantly dependent upon their experience in social life" (Simon, 1996, p. 31). Thus, there is a massive shift in the force of argument on what is appropriate in sexuality from modernism to postmodernism: from biological/scientific (mainly medical) expertise to human-rights and dignity advocacy.

3.1   THE BIRTH OF SEXOLOGY: THE SUBJECTIVITY STORY
OF SEXUALITY

Knowledge on sexuality underwent a series of fundamental historical turns from the mid-nineteenth century onwards. At the end of this the serious scientific discipline of sexology was born. It is a discipline that is now far from being exclusively medical. Its qualified representatives have medical as well as psychological, sociological and nursing backgrounds. The first medical treatises, which are strikingly naïve when viewed from the current state of art in scientific knowledge, began emerging in Germany around the turn of the nineteenth century.[3] Somewhat paradoxically, the pioneering scientific medical analyses of sexuality were mainly qualitative in nature (observations in case studies). I say paradoxically because the emerging "canon" that quickly became dominant was positivist science (represented by de Saint-Simon, Laplace and Comte and later Durkheim), which was founded on quantification and tended towards what would become known as the hypothetico-deductive model of scientific knowledge.

The pioneering German scholars who focused on sexuality were the physicians Joseph Häussler, Heinrich Kaan and Richard von Krafft-Ebing. These three men wrote books which would define the discourse on sexuality for many decades—until others, still predominantly German/Austrian scholars, with the exception of the Briton Henry Havelock Ellis, challenged their observations and arguments: Albert Moll, Sigmund Freud, Magnus Hirschfeld and Erwin J. Haeberle.

Surprisingly the emerging scientific discourses on sexuality encompassed many essential issues and complicated questions. A comprehensive look at the early scientific publications on sexuality shows that it can be broken down into several important issues that perfectly illustrate the main fears and challenges of the European sexuality-Zeitgeist at the dawn of the modern era:

1. *Ontology of sex*: is sexuality worthy of medical attention because it is integral to mental disease, or can medicine explore sex(uality) as such?
2. *Pathological vs normal*: what are the pathological aspects of sex(uality) and how much freedom is there in "normal" sexual diversity?

---

[3] A detailed overview of these historical processes is presented in Bianchi (2020).

3. *Is sexual pathology physical/essential/idiopathic or learnt/acquired:* this question is crucial when designing cures or treatments
4. *Is sexual pathology curable or not:* and if so, how?
5. *Is sex(uality) a closed/autonomous system or does it expand into other dimensions of human nature:* how is sexual subjectivity diversified in the individual?
6. *From what age does the human subject become sexual? Is there such a thing as child-sexuality?* Freud was not the only one indicating that this is the case.

Let's look at some examples of the debate on sexuality from about 150 years ago. They may give us a sense of what was shaping people's sexual subjectivity.

Ad 1: Ontology of Sex
H. Oosterhuis (2012) divides the scientific/medical emergence of sexuality into two phases. *The first phase* is acknowledging that sexual disturbances are a consequence of mental disease: "psychiatrists now took a different view, suggesting that such disturbances were actually the *cause* of sexual deviance. Their main thrust was that in many cases, irregular sexual behaviour should not be regarded as sin and crime but as symptoms of pathology. Since mental and nervous disorders often diminished responsibility, most sex offenders should not be punished but treated as patients" (Oosterhuis, 2012). The most important representative of this approach was J. Häussler, a doctor and psychiatrist from Würzburg, whose *Über die Beziehungen des Sexualsystems zur Psyche überhaupt und zum Kretenismus im Besonderen* [On the Relation of the Sexual System to the Psyche in General and to Cretinism in Particular] (1826) was a defence of the idea that sexual deviance [Abweichungen] was strongly linked to abnormal mental behaviours. The title itself leaves us in no doubt as to the link between psychiatry and sexual pathology. More interestingly, almost 200 years ago Häussler identified a mutual relationship between the psyche and the sexual system. He thought this psycho-sexual connection operated on three levels (Frame 3.1).
The second phase was largely the work of Richard von Krafft-Ebing and Albert Moll that predated that of Henry Havelock Ellis [*Studies in the Psychology of Sex* (1897–1910)] in England and Sigmund Freud [*Three Treatises on Sexual Theory,* (1905)] in Vienna and their views on sexuality.

According to Oosterhuis (2012) von Krafft-Ebing and Moll "articulated a new perspective … on sexuality in general. In the mid-1880s, Krafft-Ebing initiated the shift away from the psychiatric perspective in which deviant sexuality was explained as a derived, episodic and more or less singular symptom of a more fundamental mental disorder to it being considered a perversion that was an integral part of a more general, autonomous and continuous sexual instinct." In the 1890s, Moll elaborated on this.

Frame 3.1 Psycho-Sexual Connection Described by Häussler (1826)

1. The sexual system could be a cause of mental illness. Inappropriate sexuality and illegitimate gratification could lead to mental confusion or anger, melancholy and mental illusions. Masturbation is a particular cause of mental illness. Häussler thought the "lunatic asylum" was full of people who masturbated. But he also believed a lack of sexual satisfaction could cause disease. The result was a stronger sex drive, nymphomania, satyriasis (male hypersexuality) and melancholia.
2. Sexual stimulation could help in the treatment of mental disorders. Häussler observed how epilepsy could disappear during puberty and how other disorders were cured by pregnancy. He cited the work of Vincenzo Chiarugi (*Della pazzia, in genere, e in specie. Trattato medico-analitico, con un centuria de osservazioni,* 1793 [Trans. V. Chiarugi (1987). On Insanity and its Classification, translated with a Foreword and Introduction by G. Mora. Canton, MA: Watson Publishing International.], who allowed his psychiatric patients to have sexual intercourse for medical reasons. A recommendation Häussler was to make too, along with pregnancy for that has general health benefits.
3. Mentally ill people generally had a higher sex drive.

Ad 2: Pathological Versus Normal—Kaan and von Krafft-Ebing
Before Havelock Ellis and Freud produced their systematic description of sexual pathology, two highly influential books entitled *Psychopathia Sexualis* (Kaan, 1844; von Krafft-Ebing, 1886) were published. The introductions to both these attempt to give a "comprehensive" summary of

existing knowledge on sexuality, but in fact both concentrate on narrow, mutually contrasting ideas of "sexual psychopathy."

For Kaan, the core *psychopathia sexualis* were masturbation and (any) sexual phantasies (*onania* or *masturbatio* and *onania psychica*) (Kaan, 1844, pp. 47–48) and his Latin book was full of these. Von Krafft-Ebing, on the other hand, concentrated on "contrary sexual feelings"—in other words homosexuality—in his discussion of sexual psychopathies.

In addition to masturbation and sexual phantasies H. Kaan (1844, p. 43) mentions the following aberrations (*aberationes*) of the sex drive:

- puerorum amor (love for boys)
- amor lesbicus (lesbian love)
- violatio cadaverum (necrophilia)
- concubitus cum animalibus (zoophilia)
- expletio libidinis cum statuis (libidinal satisfaction with statues)

In his assiduous study of human sexuality, besides the pathologization of sexuality, Kaan includes a surprisingly distinctive phenomenological analysis of sexuality which, despite drawing on rather superficial observations can be seen as a contribution—especially in the long run—to the broad subjectivization of sexuality and includes a list of sexual stereotypes. In contrast to the work of Häussler (1826), Kaan identifies ten determinants of variations on a "normal" sex drive (Kaan, 1844, p. 42):

1. Women find sex more enriching than men do.
2. Differences given by temperament (choleric and sanguine individuals have the highest sex drives).
3. Differences given by physical constitution.
4. Diminished sex drive due to progressive diseases.
5. Differences in sex drive caused by nutrition style.
6. Sex drive varies according to season (highest in spring and summer).
7. Climatic influence (sex drive is highest in hot regions, lower in moderate climates and low in Nordic regions).
8. Race: the highest sex drive is found in *Aethiopibus* (African), while it is lower in *Mongolica* (Asian) and lowest in *Caucasica* (Caucasian) people.
9. Lifestyle: sex drive is higher in rural agricultural communities and lower in city inhabitants.
10. Altering sex drive: moderate exercise arouses sexual and reproductive instincts; excessive sex results in later weakness.

Ad 3: Is Sexual Pathology Physical/Essential/Idiopathic or Learnt/Acquired?
The early debate among sexuality scholars on the causes of sexual deviation was cautious, given the absence of knowledge about hormones,
genetics and the brain, and this is aptly illustrated by Freud's thinking
about the causality of homosexuality in the first of his *Three Essays on the
Theory of Sexuality – The Sexual Aberrations (1905)*. Freud distinguishes
between absolute inversion (homosexuality), amphigenous inversion
(bisexuality) and occasional inversion and thought both causes of homosexuality—inherited or acquired (mainly due to a traumatic episode in
early childhood associated with the failure to handle the Oedipus complex). Freud thought absolute inversion, bisexuality and occasional homosexuality were inherited. He found it hard to imagine there was no
"learning" effect/acquisition based on life experience. Freud ended this
debate cautiously, stating that neither of the two causes of homosexuality
could be excluded and that neither on its own was sufficient explanation
of homosexuality.

Ad 4: Is Sexual Pathology Curable?
Surprisingly, even back in 1844 there were various cures for sexual problems. Kaan in his *Psychopathia sexualis* (1944) wrote about *Curandi meth-
odus psychica; physica; diaetetica. Therapia radicalis*. Under *therapia
psychica* Kaan includes rational therapy, music therapy, religious therapy
and moral therapy (part of which is getting married or being married).

Ad 5: Is Sex(uality) a Closed/Autonomous System?
In the introduction to his *Psychopathia Sexualis*, "Fragments of a system of
psychology of sexual life," von Krafft-Ebing (1886) writes about a range
of sexual contexts—the societal, moral and political contexts of sexuality:
the differences between male and female sexuality, the relationship
between morality and sexuality, and even the intrusion of sexuality in politics and the associated risks for political and public life. In light of what we
now know, some of his comments almost seem ridiculous; nonetheless, his
medical (scientific) authority and courage in writing about sexuality led to
certain attitudes becoming deeply rooted—the negative consequences of
which we have yet to deal with; this applies especially to the two diametric
views of male and female sexuality and the socio-political consequences:

> In the sexual demands of man's nature will be found the motives of his
> weakness towards woman. He is enslaved by her, and becomes more and
> more dependent upon her as he grows weaker, and the more he yields to

sensuality. This accounts for the fact that in the periods of decline and luxury sensuousness was the predominant factor. From this arises the social danger where courtesans and their dependents rule the State and finally encompass its ruin. (von Krafft-Ebing, 1886/1965, p. 9)

The "innocence" of the male sexual role and women's "guilt" when it comes to unfaithfulness is described thus by von Krafft-Ebing:

From the fact that by nature man plays the aggressive role in sexual life, he is exposed to the danger of overstepping the limits set by law and morality. The unfaithfulness of the wife, as compared with that of the husband, is morally of much wider bearing, and should always meet with severer punishment at the hands of the law. The unfaithful wife not only dishonours herself, but also her husband and her family, not to speak of possible uncertainty of paternity. Natural instincts and social position are frequent causes of disloyalty in man (the husband), whilst the wife is surrounded by many protecting influences. (von Krafft-Ebing, 1886/1965, p. 9)

Notwithstanding the above, von Krafft-Ebing was surprisingly empathetic and liberal in his psychological thinking, casting doubt on the point of celibacy:

It shows a masterly psychological knowledge of human nature that the Roman Catholic Church enjoins celibacy for its priests in order to emancipate them from sensuality, and to concentrate their entire activity in the pursuit of their calling. Nevertheless it is a pity that the celibate state deprives the priest of the ennobling influence exercised by love and marital life upon the character. (von Krafft-Ebing, 1886/1965, p. 9)

Ad 6: Child-Sexuality

Two thirds of the *Three Essays on the Theory of Sexuality* by Sigmund Freud (published first in 1905) are devoted to child-sexuality and its development through puberty. For Freud early sexuality—from the oral stage in siblings to anal and genital sexuality (including children's predisposition for polymorphic perversity)—was the essence of his theory of personality (and subjectivity), and of his search for the aetiology of mental problems. Freud's work was followed by that of Albert Moll, the second scholar to publish a separate volume on child-sexuality. His earlier work on sexuality generally was originally published in German [*Research into the Libido Sexualis*] in 1897–1898, but his *Das Sexualleben des Kindes [The Sexual Life of the Child]* was not published until 1908 (1912 in English). As Moll was a complex character and did not found his own school, his work was soon forgotten. Consequently Freud's legacy on early sexuality in children was still much in evidence in the twenty-first century, influencing our ideas and fears of child-sexuality and thus the subjectivity of child-sexuality itself.

Whatever the positive aspects of the early medical nineteenth-century treatises on sexuality, we have without doubt paid and indeed still are paying a high price for the fact that sexuality became a topic of scientific/medical interest. This interest was justified by the emphasis on disease and deviation which required treatment—a traditional concern in medicine. Paradoxically, the most influential pioneer, who has exerted a strong influence on sexual discourse up until the present day, was Sigmund Freud, whose primary interest was not sexuality but human personality. For Freud sexuality was just a way and means of fully understanding the nature and structure of human personality and its role in the treatment of neuroses. Recovering from more than a hundred years of the nosocomial pathologization of sexuality is beset with obstacles thrown up by post-secular movements (Vattimo, 2002; Rorty & Vattimo, 2007; Caputo et al., 2007) and the great renaissance of conservative power. Some call the current tension a "culture war," but it is more like an institutional war between the organizations that emerged after the Second World War (e.g. International Planned Parenthood Federation with its general policy on Sexual and Reproductive Health and Rights—SRHR) and regional and local religious institutions (Bishops' Conferences, Christian NGOs, etc.) with authoritative backing from the Vatican.

3.2   Words, Texts, Their Tectonics
and the Sexual Subject

This chapter is about the search for sexual subjectivity in discourses. But first we have to begin by taking a few steps back in order to explain the textual background of psychology. This requires us to return to Chap. 1 and the discussion on the role of text/discourse in defining/determining human subjectivity.

Readers may remember Gergen (1998), who insisted on a textual definition of "the person," highlighting the diversity of textual representations of one and the same person—in culture, scientific discourse and the laboratory.

> The psychological subject is pre-eminently a textual being, born of a confluence of discursive practices. (Gergen, 1998, p. 111)

Hence our knowledge of the "person who is the focus of the study" results from "multiple-coding" in texts/discourses.

Brown and Stenner (2009) warn against simplification: "the psychological is not thinkable without linguistic mediation, and yet neither is it reducible to language" (Brown & Stenner, 2009, p.7). Moreover, we need to take the contextual aspects into account: the external contexts of the subject that refer to history and culture (e.g. Gergen), power (e.g. Foucault), language and discourse (e.g. Potter) or the dynamics of the unconscious (e.g. Lacan). And, as Curt (1994) captures, is topologically, between the "inner" subject and the "outer" contexts of power/institutions/ideology/things there are the discourses and their tectonics.

Foucault questions, but does not reject, the idea that texts/discourses/their tectonics are important for human subjectivity, in opining that subjectivation is not the result of "free play with signs" (in texts) (Alvesson & Skölberg, ibid., p. 148), that the subject is "not primarily a social construction, but a construction of the self reflecting on the self" (ibid, p.230). Foucault considers the active role of the self to be crucial—"technologies of self"[4]—the instruments/operations which make being a subject possible. The discursive material is, however, present, important and active.

By drawing a simplified, mechanical comparison with *content* versus *form* dualism, the text/discourse can be understood as constitutive of diverse contents vis-à-vis the subject, whereas the self-creating actor role of the self gives the subject its "final shape."

In a recent publication (Bianchi, 2020) I presented a comprehensive structure of sexuality-relevant discourses.[5] So here I will introduce it

---

[4] There are four kinds of technologies, according to Foucault (1988/2000): (1) production technologies, (2) technologies of signs, meanings and symbols, (3) technologies of power determining the agency of individuals, leading to subordination to certain goals and control by others and resulting in the objectification of the subject and (4) technologies of the self-enabling individual agency.

[5] It was not until the focal ontological and epistemic shift in social science and the humanities that followed the linguistic turn in the use of language in social interaction that the full potential of qualitative research on sexuality could be exploited. People use discourses to attribute guilt, apologize, portray themselves in a positive light, etc. (Gill, 2003a). Discourses are important because meanings, norms, values and identities are created through mutual communicative interaction between people and institutions. Discourses are basically the semantic spaces within which we live, plan, evaluate and become ourselves and part of the desired social setting. The current discourses of sexuality frame our discussions about sexual health, sexual satisfaction and the risks associated with sex.

briefly (with one additional category) in order to outline the potential diversity in the figurations of human sexual subjectivity.

> **Discourses on sexuality can be identified on at least five levels/ categories:**
>
> 1. The historical perspective[6] (vertical linearity of time)
> 2. A cross-cultural perspective (horizontal geographical distribution) of cultural diversity—e.g. between the Eastern and Western world represented by Jainism, Buddhism and Hinduism on the one hand and Christianity on the other hand: with their acceptance of erotica, sexual pleasure-seeking and the satisfaction of sexual needs versus the self-denial of mundane aspects of life en route to enlightenment.[7]
> 3. Issue-targeted discourses (discourses on sex work, pornography, LGBTQ, sexuality education, risk, etc.)
> 4. Current living/active (general) discourses on sexuality in a particular cultural space.
> 5. Inter-generation/education discourses.

---

[6] Regarding the historical perspective on sexuality discourse development (vertical linearity of time), Domna C. Stanton (1992) edited a comprehensive overview entitled *Discourses of sexuality: From Aristotle to AIDS* (1992). The studies focus on the Western world. Stanton's selection of studies by prominent authors includes a critical reflection on parts of Michel Foucault's iconic four volumes of the *History of Sexuality* and highlights the historical continuity and dynamics in determining subjectivity related to sexuality (pleasure, sexual desire, gender, body, birth, sexual inversions, etc). As Stanton states, it is important to have a historical perspective on sexuality: "Freud rejected or ignored the historicity of sexual practices and categories as well as their cultural specificity, which Mary Douglas has underscored: nothing is more essentially transmitted by a social process of learning than sexual behavior" (Stanton, 1992, pp. 3–4). In historical perspectives all conceptualizations are interlinked. Furthermore Lesley Dean-Jones' "The Politics of Pleasure" (1992, pp. 48–78), highlights both the importance of the interrelations between historical periods (classical Greek vs Christianity) and of constructing and understanding sexual morphology, gender-stereotypes, discrimination, self-discipline, sexual agency, pleasure seeking and culture and sexual norms.

[7] Compare, e.g. Dalrymple (2009/2017).

Both the historical and cross-cultural perspectives create discourses which inevitably permeate the cultural/societal syntax of sexual scripts (Simon, 1996) used by sexual subjects in sexual bargaining. Thus the values of participating individuals' sexual subjectivity are a combination of successive milestones: the Ancient World, Christianity, Enlightenment, the emergence of civil and political rights, science and positivism, the social and human rights agenda, reproductive advances (hormonal contraception, artificial reproductive techniques (ART)) and feminisms. At the same time, they are facilitated by globalization and the internet; hence we need to include a strong cross-cultural perspective (horizontal geographical distribution of cultural diversity—e.g. between the Eastern and Western world with all the religious and secular platforms).

While the *historical and cultural discourses* on sexuality are primarily "owned" and exploited by groups sharing similar values (including churches, political parties and civil society, NGOs representing certain value-based positions), *issue-targeted discourses* (discourses on sex work, pornography, LGBTQ, sex education, abortion, risk, etc.) serve institutions, professional associations, researchers and policy-making processes in the first instance and are used in the subjectivity constructions of the persons concerned. Finally, the sexuality discourses that ordinary people are most directly influenced by fall into the last two categories: *current living/ active (general) discourses* on sexuality. In a particular cultural space/time in the "Western world," these are:[8]

1. The Christian tradition discourses
2. Scientific, medical and sexology discourses
3. Civic liberal discourses
4. The pragmatic discourse (originating in the *risks of HIV/AIDS* discourse)

The intergenerational/education discourses are generated in face-to-face communication in core social units—the family, school settings (teacher–child, peers). These discourses provide the constituents of the dyadic syntax in sexual scripts (Simon, 1996), and, as A. Čierna (2021a, b)

---

[8] The four discourses are from Supeková et al. (1998) and are based on the work of Foucault (1990/1976/1979) and Gagnon and Parker (1995), described in detail in Bianchi (2020).

has recently shown in Slovakia, in general there are three such discourses between parents and elementary school children: (1) open parent–child discussions on any topic, (2) strict/restricted question/answer dialogues that are impersonal (non-committal), which are directed specifically at the child's questions and refer only to other people's sexuality and (3) a separate discourse on sexual violence.

In relation to sexual subjectivity it is necessary to highlight the mutual interactions of all these horizontally and vertically organized discourses which constitute the discursive tectonics in the sense of Beryl Curt's (1994) distinction between textuality and tectonics. Thus if an individual person strives to understand its sexual subjectivity she needs to take a stand on most of them and their mutual interactions that grow out of value antagonisms most of all.

Along with this complex categorization of specific levels of discourse (and their "content") outlined above, there is also a very productive view of the differences among discourses from a historical-epistemological perspective. Agnieszka Borowiak (2001) has highlighted formal distinctions between pre-modern, modern and postmodern discourses generally. If we consider these as dimensions of subjectivity creation, the differences between them concern (1) three cognitive categories: "capacity to decentrate" (remember Piaget), "method of validation of knowledge," "subjective vs. objective orientation"; (2) two value-based categories: "locus of control over individual development," "attitudes towards time dimensions"; as well as (3) one content category: "source of personal identity" (see Table 3.1). Thus the specific type of discourse, when placed in one of the three categories (pre-modern, modern, postmodern), is obvious to determine its users subjectivity regarding his/her flexibility of cognitive argumentation, need for method to validate the opinion, focus on the naïve-objective-or-subjective, belief in sources of subjectivity and referential values (of control-authority and target location in time past–future–present).

3.3   Subjectivity of Sexual Performance

3.3.1   Subjective Meaning of Sex

As I outlined in Bianchi (2020), quantitative correlational and/or experimental studies have offered several relatively complex categorizations of the various meanings of sex. However, most of these are narrowly targeted and tend to focus mainly on gender differences. One of the earliest studies

Table 3.1 Three types of discourse (Agnieszka Borowiak, 2001)

	Capacity to decentrate	Method of knowledge validation	Subjective vs objective orientation	Control over individual development	Personal identity	Attitudes to time—what is most important
Pre-modern Traditional	Low	No need	Naïve realism	Fate	Inheritance	Past
Modern Rational	Medium	Logical	Objective orientation	Law	Self-cognition	Future
Postmodern Relativistic	High	Fragmentary	Subjective orientation	Contingency	Self-creation	Present

confirming the importance of the subjective meaning of sex was by Libby and Straus (1980). It showed that the subjective meaning of sex had an intervening effect on the interaction between sexual arousal and aggression—the fate of competing hypotheses—"the more sex, the more violence" and "the more sex, the less violence." The authors found that the first hypothesis was valid if the subjective meaning of sex followed the *traditional male stereotype* of sex as a dominant and exploitative act, and conversely that the second hypothesis was valid if the subjective meaning of sex was a *warm, affectionate act*; however, this intervening effect on the relationship between sexual arousal and violence only works in men. Murstein and Turkheimer (1998), Sprague and Quadagno (1989), and Vanwesenbeeck et al. (1998) looked at the meaning of sex from different perspectives and identified diverse categories. Murstein and Turkheimer: (1) sex associated with intimacy and the relationship, (2) sex to gain experience, (3) sex as relaxation and adventure and (4) sex as a necessity, whether out of a need for self-satisfaction or self-affirmation; Sprague and Quadagno: (1) a physical motive, (2) a love motive, (3) to please a partner and (4) the fear of abandonment—the physical motive being more frequent in men than women; Vanwesenbeeck et al.: (1) sensation seeking, (2) sexual compulsiveness and (3) sexual anxiety—male respondents reported more sexual compulsion and more sexual sensation seeking, while women reported more sexual anxiety.

Since the emergence of discursive psychology in the late 1980s little qualitative research has been performed on the (various) *subjective meanings of sex*: what sex means to people. However, this research has substantially improved our understanding of human sexual subjectivity. Based on substantial theoretical background of the discursive approach and discourse analysis in psychology (Potter et al., 1990; Willig, 1993) the importance of identifying subjective meanings expressed in discourse becomes more evident. Why? In a discursive paradigm meanings operate within the interpretative repertoire of activities implicit in the "object of interest" (sex). The interpretative repertoire includes the subject/actor's social/ psychological position in the interactive situation, as well as the "actor's" subjectivity/identity. Therefore, the subjective meaning of sex identified in qualitative research may capture the actor's genuine subjectivity and reflect interindividual differences determined by, among other things, schematic dichotomies of operationalized "independent variables" (e.g.

the respondent's gender). It therefore has a much stronger predictive impact on how the actor's sexual interactions develop.

Based on previous research, Ingham et al. (1996) produced a fixed codebook for analysing in-depth interviews in a European comparative research project on heterosexual conduct and HIV. It contained a list of 25 subjective meanings of sex: a goal in and of itself, coupled with love/intimacy, sex leads to intimacy, intimacy leads to sex, personal pleasure, pleasing the other, self-confirmation, sex is natural—a part of life, excitement—adventure—"the kick," the "hunt," contact with the other, experimentation, rebellion, obligation, warmth—affection—cosiness, comfort, forgetting—escapism, relaxation, fear and feeling threatened, achievement, romance, establishing relationship, maintaining relationship, surrendering—"letting go," and so on.

In this comparative qualitative study exploring young people's sex careers in Slovakia (Supeková et al., 2005; 15 women and 15 men, aged 18–32 years) participants generated complex meanings of sex. Four categories of meaning occurred most frequently (repeatedly) during the process of searching in the transcripts of the interviews for the narrow meanings suggested by Ingham et al. (above). These were:

1. Sex is essential to and inseparable from the partnership, intimacy and love. It is a view of sex that relegates it to being a subordinate component of the evolving partnership and intimate relationship. The importance of the relationship prevails over the meaning (and value) of sex. Sex without or outside the partner relationship is inconceivable.
2. Sex is about personal enjoyment and satisfaction (sex is a source of excitement, experimentation and satisfaction). Hedonism is the dominant factor—intimate consumerism. Being in an emotionally satisfying relationship may improve the quality of the sex, but it is not essential.
3. Sex is more about the partner's enjoyment than one's enjoyment. Here the person has less need for sexual satisfaction and, for various reasons, engages in sex as a means of developing and maintaining the partner relationship. Sex is determined by the other person's needs.
4. Sex is a means of improving one's self-image, self-confirmation (the ability to gain a sexual partner is a source of self-affirmation, and leads to the feeling of personal success). This view of sex is typical of the "hunters" who find satisfaction in the act of continually gaining

new sexual partners.[9] The criterion for satisfaction is not sex itself but gaining the approval of sexual partners. Someone who follows this kind of script is typically implicitly and permanently dissatisfied in their relationships—they are only seeking a partner for sex, and lose interest in that partner once they have obtained the sex and further satisfaction can only be achieved through the pursuit for a new partner.

The first two categories feature in findings by Olmstead et al. (2018) from their research in college students ($N = 268$). They conducted a semi-qualitative study and identified three groups of participants with different sex life patterns:

1. Committers—more commonly women than men (they consider sex to be indicative of love and trust and it occurs once they are committed to the relationship),
2. Flexibles—more commonly men (the sex may have a deep personal meaning, but it may also be purely for pleasure and isn't always connected to commitment), and
3. Recreationers—more commonly men (sex is a basic need or is purely for pleasure and is not associated with commitment).

However, Olmstead, Anders and Conrad did not find the remaining two categories of the subjective meaning of sex: "altruistic" "partner's enjoyment" and "self-confirmation."

In our study (Supeková & Bianchi, 2000; Supeková et al., 2005) we examined the *relationships between the subjective meaning of sex, sex life*

---

[9] Recently evidence was found on the universal validity of a pattern called mate poaching, which relates to these "hunters" who continually search for new sexual partner. This research enlightens the ease accompanying scenarios for finding new sexual partners (Schmitt et al., 2004b). Patterns of mate poaching are universally valid across more than 50 cultures and on each continent. Schmitt et al. found that a very high percentage of people actively seek to "steal" a sexual partner from someone else. In men the percentage is 56.9% and 57.1% for one-off sex and long-term relationship or to produce off-spring respectively, and in women it is 34.9% and 43.6%, respectively. On average globally the prevalence of mate poaching is 2.32 and 2.42 efforts in males (one-off sex and long-term relationship or to produce offspring respectively) and 1.68 and 1.94 in women (one-off sex and long-term relationship or to produce off-spring respectively). More importantly though, these attempts are largely successful: in each of the two conditions, and both for men and women, the success rate is above 80%.

patterns, sexual satisfaction, and the desires and visions of young hetero-sexual adults with experience of multiple sexual partners. The analysis was part of a genuine search for complex sexual subjectivity. We found that subjective meanings of sex are closely linked to the person's type of sexual relationship, sexual scenarios (i.e. what they do during sex) and sexual satisfaction or dissatisfaction. Efforts to achieve sexual satisfaction (sexual motivation) are strongly related to the subjective meaning of sex. Thus, participants in a steady monogamous relationship predominantly localized their subjective meaning of sex as being tied up with *love and intimacy,* participants with both steady and casual sexual partners identified sex with *personal pleasure* and *self-confirmation,* and participants not in a steady relationship had sex as *self-confirmation* (when not looking for a steady relationship) or perceived sex as with *love/intimacy* (if looking for a steady relationship but not getting the opportunity). Participants whose subjective meaning of sex fell in the first category (*love and intimacy*) were most satisfied with their sex life. Paradoxically, these people may feel sexually satisfied even when they don't have sex with their partner for several months or have no partner. This is the only group of people who are paradoxically "sexually happy even when not having sex," as assumed by Golombok and Rust (1983). The complexity of sexual subjectivity in sexual performance concerns also the number of sexual partners. The highest number of sexual partners was reported by participants who were not in a steady partnership (and not seeking one) and who related sex to self-confirmation. The lowest number of partners was reported by those in steady monogamous partnerships, who related sex to love/intimacy. Another important finding was that for participants for whom sex had the subjective meaning of *personal enjoyment* and *improvement of self-image* there was no simple linear relationship between the number of sexual partners, sexual acts or experiences on the one hand and the level of sexual satisfaction on the other: consumption of sexual episodes does not directly increase sexual satisfaction. Moreover, this group of participants had a much lower overall level of sexual satisfaction than those for whom sex was about *intimacy and love.*

Until now the discussion on the meaning of sex has been limited to straight/heterosexual sex. So the question is: what does *sex mean to MSM* (men who have sex with men)? In European research designed to obtain information on the health risks for MSM,[10] I identified four categories of subjective meanings of sex in the Slovak sample that match some of the heterosexual meanings, but also reflect the specific nature of MSM relationships (Frame 3.2).

Frame 3.2 Meaning of Sex for MSM:

Category 1. "gay people want a monogamous relationship – just as many heterosexuals do" (sex = part of the relationship; a heteronormative conceptualization).

Category 2. Sex as a means whereby the two lovers achieve equality, where that equality is expressed in terms of disease/suffering. Voluntarily exposing oneself to the "deadly" risk of catching HIV from a HIV+ partner. This story illustrates the strong conceptual link between the sex and the relationship, but it is based on an extreme experience and differs from Category 1, partly because it is not dependent on the heteronormative pattern.

Category 3. Some participants repeatedly stated that some sexual activities (e.g. mutual masturbation) were "ontologically" different from penetrative sex, that the moral implications of sex between MSM on faithfulness differed from those of "heterosexual infidelity," and that extra-relational sex was compatible with a faithful relationship (sexual activities performed for variety outside a functioning long-term relationship between two gay men).

Category 4. One of the less sexually experienced participants talked of having "heard" about unprotected sex. His narrative is illustrative of the variety and ambiguity in opinions and views of safe sex. He had had a number of relationships (including stable ones) but it was not until much later, based on new information, that he began thinking about having unprotected sex.

---

[10] The research was conducted as part of Sialon, an international project involving seven central and southern European countries investigating the nature of health risks for MSM. In-depth interviews about the participants' sex lives were held with 21 men (half of whom were aged 24–53) who had had sex with other men. Parts of the research were published earlier in Bianchi (2010b). This research is discussed in greater detail in Bianchi (2020).

In the MSM population, sex has meanings that have not been identified in the heterosexual population (e.g. sex as a means of achieving a "moral" counterbalance to one's partner's disease; ontological distinctions between various sexual activities; parallel compatible sexual scenarios). The most important finding relating to the search for human sexual subjectivity is that "heteronormative aspirations" may influence/reinforce a monogamous sex script in MSM. Hence there is a duality of specific sexual subjectivity features in MSM and common features arising from the normative overlaps between the heterosexual and homosexual arenas.

While most sexuality studies have focused on young people, or young adults, the *sexuality of elderly people* has begun attracting scientific attention. Bianca Fileborn and her team (Fileborn et al., 2018) explored the meanings sex acquires for *heterosexual men aged 60 and over*. Their study shows that their experiences do not easily fit into the "decline" and "success" narratives of ageing. On the contrary, intimacy with a well-structured sexual subjectivity may be central to the sex lives of elderly men.

There are (at least) another four aspects relating to sexual subjectivity: sexual satisfaction, the motives behind sexual interactions, "managing" the boundary between wanted and unwanted in sex and ways of coping with risk in sexual interactions.

3.3.2   Sexual Satisfaction

In Bianchi (2020) I outlined changes in conceptualizations of *sexual satisfaction*, drawing on the work of Sigmund Freud, through H. Ellis, A. Kinsey, W.H. Masters and V.E. Johnson, S.S. Hacker (in Ansuini et al., 1996), Golombok and Rust (1983), Valent (1989), Laumann et al. (1996), Moret et al. (1998), Haavio-Mannila et al. (1997), Flowers et al. (1997) and Young and Luquis (1998). I then suggested that the conceptualization of sexual satisfaction can be tentatively summarized in the following classification of the many potential sources that give rise to the phenomenological plurality of sexual satisfaction experiences that contribute to the potential diversity of sexual subjectivity (Frame 3.3):

Frame 3.3 Possible Sources and Experiences of Sexual Satisfaction:

1. Being satisfied with your sexuality: having a balanced view of the sexual experiences you've had in your life.
2. Being satisfied with your partner/interaction: degree of sexual satisfaction is determined by both partners taking part in, being active in, and achieving satisfaction during sexual interactions.
3. Being satisfied with the relationship: being in a permanent relationship can be important for subjective feelings of sexual satisfaction.
4. Satisfaction through giving: feeling positive about your partner, affection and taking an active part in sex can be a source of subjective feelings of sexual satisfaction.
5. Satisfaction through receiving: accepting positive emotions and affection from your partner may be part of the subjective experience of sexual satisfaction.
6. Achieving individual physical sexual satisfaction—pleasure and sexual release.

3.3.3   Sexual Debut

Sexual Debut

Another aspect of sexual subjectivity can be found in a person's *sexual debut*—the key event in a sexual career in a number of ways. It is important to the future development of subsequent sex life, as has been highlighted by, among others, Weiss et al. (1996), "Many findings indicate that first experience of sexual intercourse is one of the factors that frequently and substantially affects the subsequent sexual life course." Bozon and Kontula (1998, p. 38) state that first sexual intercourse has "always been considered a crucial stage in the individual's life history and *self-construction*." Most of the research in this area is in the form of quantitative surveys, which do not enable deep and broad understanding of sexual initiation.

Age of Sexual Debut

In Bianchi (2020) I provided an exhaustive overview of age of coitarche (first intercourse) in Europe. Over time there have been important shifts in coitarche that can be related to contextual factors. Average/median age used to be lower in men than women, but that has changed. Using data from West-European countries Bozon and Kontula state that (1) there was not a massive decrease in coitarche age during the second half of the twentieth century in Western Europe, and (2) "the reduction in age at sexual initiation that occurred over the second half of the twentieth century was more marked for women than for men" (Bozon & Kontula, 1998, p. 40). These findings from Western Europe can be contrasted with data from Eastern Europe to highlight the cultural/political/societal context. In a comparative study in seven post-socialist countries in central and southern Europe in 1997, the researchers expected to find a higher prevalence of sexually initiated teenagers (aged 17–18 years) in post-socialist countries than in western Germany and Austria but could not confirm their delayed modernity hypothesis (Bernik & Hlebec, 2005). Primary reflexivity[11] was evidently already regulating the start of an active sex life. Primary and secondary reflexivity is a useful concept for pinpointing the interactive way in which sexual subjectivity is constructed—whether and how cultural/political/societal influences are processed in the diversified figurations of sexual subjectivity.

Why should we be interested in the age at which young people start their active sex life? What is the relationship between that and their future sexual subjectivity? Bozon and Kontula found in their meta-analytical study of surveys in several European countries that "early entry to adult sexuality marks the start of a well-identified sexual career characterized by more sexual partners, a more diverse sexual repertoire and some distance from couple and family issues... [however]... in the female population, differences between sexual lifestyles are ... less connected to the age at first intercourse... [but also, citing Bajos et al., 1998]...early starters [may] lead 'riskier' lives but are perhaps characterized by greater adaptability to risk" (Bozon & Kontula, 1998, p. 62). In Slovakia (15 is the age of consent) we found that an early sexual debut (under the age of 16) often has negative consequences; people whose first sexual intercourse is before the age of 16 are statistically more likely to have a riskier sexual career. For example, they may have a large number of sexual partners, or a large

---

[11] Primary and secondary reflexivity is the "response to risks associated with sexual activity and to double standards of sexual morality" (primary reflexivity) and the "redefinition of sexual roles in high modern societies, which brings more communicativeness, openness and negotiation into sexual interaction (secondary reflexivity) (Bernik & Hlebec, 2005, p. 304). The authors expect primary reflexivity to be more pronounced in women (higher health "stakes" of sexual interaction) and that secondary reflexivity (mainly facilitates women's emancipatory agency) will affect both women and men equally.

number of casual sexual partners, and may suffer from substance addiction (Lukšík, 2003; Lukšík et al., 1998).

Sexual Debut Motives
Qualitative research revealing sexual debut motives has produced other insights. Besides the "basic" question of the most frequently mentioned motives, another important question is the *gender differences in sexual debut motives* that reflect the way gender stereotypes and gender roles interact and contribute to sexual subjectivity. Findings from a comparative study (Bianchi, 2020; Popper et al., 2005) show that in Slovakia, only two of the five most common motives—curiosity and opportunity/right circumstances—were mentioned equally by men and women. The other frequently mentioned motives (reaching a sexual stage where having intercourse would be natural), opportunity—a suitable partner ("finally there was someone [to do it with]" and "lust" (sexual appetite/libido)) were primary motives for men. "Typical female" motives, those mentioned more frequently by women than by men, were: (1) being in a serious relationship, (2) natural progression of the relationship, (3) feeling it was right, as well as (4) emotional blackmail from the partner and (5) partner pressure. This marked gender difference in motives for first sexual intercourse confirms Bernik and Hlebec's (2005) premise relating to primary reflexivity in sexuality. Primary reflexivity enables women to protect themselves from the negative consequences of male sexual impulsiveness and probably determines female sexual subjectivity.

We can also consider sexual debut in terms of cross-cultural comparisons of the motives behind it. As Michel Hubert points out, "the meaning, range, and content of what we class as sexual, are far from shared by all societies" (Hubert, 1998, p. 4). We can therefore ask whether Slovakia is different or typical in any way. Are the most frequent motives among young Slovaks the same as those among young people in the Netherlands or the UK? Is sexual debut "driven" by universal (biological or social) forces or by something that is culturally specific? In William Simon's (1996) language this would be cultural versus intrapsychic (and possibly vs dyadic) scripting of the sexual subject's sexual debut.

The strongest cross-cultural similarity we found was the sexual debut motive of personal success ("I can do it") and loss of virginity; both of which were reported equally by men and women, but these were, in general, among the less frequent motives.

Then there were the motives that were common to both the Slovak participants and either the Dutch participants (a "natural part of sexual development" and "feeling it was right") or the UK participants (direct peer pressure, indirect pressure of feeling it was a social duty, and physical attraction).

Bearing in mind the gradual formation of sexual subjectivity, these findings can be interpreted as having potential implications for sex education: greater attention should be paid to the sexual debut motives that we might call culturally specific sexual debut motives. These were either much more or much less frequent among young Slovaks than in the other countries and were (1) being emotionally blackmailed by partner, (2) "lust," (3) opportunity—the right circumstances ("finally there's somewhere [to do it]") and (4) opportunity—a suitable partner ("finally there's someone [to do it with]"). The first was more typical among women and the other three were more typical of men (Bianchi, 2020; Popper et al., 2005). When considering how we could shift sexual subjectivity towards healthy sex, it is clear that the main points Slovakia needs to focus on are: (1) the rigid expectations regarding male and female gender roles, which make it easier for partners to engage in emotional blackmail, (2) the general conformity evident in various kinds of pressure and finally (3) impulsiveness and situatedness/incidentality.

Going Beyond Incongruent Sexual Scripts on Sexual Debut
Given the differences in sexual scripts (Simon, 1996) between the (two) actors considering sexual interaction there is also the issue of possible dyadic negotiation. Thus, the two partners may gain the opportunity to integrate their potentially incongruent cultural/societal scripts and individual intrapsychic sexual expectations/determinations. The dialogue could evolve into a joint dyadic script. I showed above that comparing "male" and "female" motives leads into a complex and dynamic area of the dialogue that may take place between the two sexual subjects before first sex happens. For young men and women to engage in a sexual debut that is both satisfying and safe, the risk of pregnancy is another issue that should be discussed. In our comparative study (Bianchi, 2020; Popper et al., 2005) 43% of participants in Slovakia reported that no communication took place before sex and 23% reported engaging in communication "to some extent." Just 33% reported having a proper conversation about the possible risks (and 37% actually took measures to prevent pregnancy), whereas in the Dutch sample 50% entered into discussion (and 73% took measures to prevent pregnancy). The percentages for the UK sample were most disappointing (51% did not communicate at all and only 23% stated

that they had a proper conversation about the possible risks. Data from this qualitative research also shows that there was no secondary reflexivity (Bernik & Hlebec, 2005)—in contrast to primary reflexivity. Conversations about sexual interaction were strongly determined by gender stereotypes and did not include women's autonomy. Important gender differences in sexual debut motivations and triggers are confirmed by extensive quantitative data analysed by Bozon and Kontula. They concluded that "In spite of the general reduction of gender differences, men and women still differ in all countries by the value they attach to first intercourse and first partner" (Bozon & Kontula, 1998, p. 61).

Parents, Children and Sexual Debut
One possible explanation for this persistent gender imbalance may lie in "vertical" transfer within the family, whereby traditional ideas about asymmetric gender-based roles continue to exert a greater influence in Slovakia and this is reflected in sexual subjectivity. It can also be explained by comparing conversations about sex with parents. In Slovakia 57% of participants reported hardly any or no conversations (in the Netherlands 45%) and 0% of participants reported open conversations (in the Netherlands 25%). Moreover, in Slovakia 83% of participants reported predominantly implicit communication (in the Netherlands 63% reported predominantly explicit communication). Implicit communication is similar to "no communication"—it basically confirms rigid stereotypical acts and the avoidance of deliberation.[12]

Parent–child discussions on sexuality can be considered in relation to parenting style. In this research, clear distinctions were identified in the parenting approaches in the various cultures. While the majority of the Dutch participants considered their upbringing to be permissive, most of the Slovak participants thought their upbringing was restrictive and repressive. In the UK, the largest share of participants thought their upbringing had been neither strictly permissive nor repressive but "mixed" and ambivalent (this applied to more than a third of the sample) (Popper et al., 2005; Supeková et al., 2005). One could therefore conclude that in Slovakia parental discussions with children about sexuality are likely to be

---

[12] The limited communication between parents and children in Slovakia is compensated for by frequent communication with friends. In Slovakia 53% and 63% of participants often talk to their friends about relationships and the physical aspects of sex, respectively, whereas in the Netherlands the percentage is significantly lower—27% and 34%.

(1) restrictive and repressive, (2) lacking in openness and (3) indirect (implicitly reinforcing traditional stereotypes).

All these findings correspond to Bozon and Kontula's (1998) general statement that "Despite these (some) common trends, it cannot be maintained that a European sex culture with regard to first sexual intercourse has arisen. From one country to the other, the starting points as well as the time and extent of changes have been variable, and, as a result, different patterns of relations between men and women at sexual initiation have been observed" (Bozon & Kontula, 1998, p. 60).

3.3.4 Coping with Taboos, Sins, Risks[13] and Their Justifications

There is a direct link between risk and several key normative aspects of sexuality—health, social, moral and legal norms. When seeking sexual satisfaction people are often tempted to experiment with dangerous, unwanted or forbidden acts. Sexual subjectivity is therefore also about these dangerous, unwanted or forbidden aspects—*How much do I want that and why?*, *How do I decide?*, *What would be the consequences of doing (or not doing) that?* etc.

As I showed and described in detail earlier (Bianchi, 2020) three dominant discourses regulate our thinking about these adverse aspects of sexual performance—taboo, sin and risk. These discourses, or epistemological platforms for assessing dangerous and unwanted behaviour, have emerged as human cognition has evolved over history (Wiedemann, 1992): (1) the first discourse appeared in the era of animistic and totemist thinking, (2) the second during the transition from animism towards deism and the emergence of religious morality, as part of thinking that was still largely magical and/or analogical, symbolic and personified rather than correlational (thus precluding genuine causal thinking) and therefore tolerant of logical contradictions (e.g. the Catholic Church recommending the use of "natural" contraceptive methods, yet rejecting barrier ones) and (3) the third during the Enlightenment when the concept of (mathematically computable) risk appeared that embodied "the curse of freedom of decision-making" that faces anyone rationally calculating the likelihood of a decision having undesirable consequences. Once pure causality thinking became possible and mathematical probability was discovered, the notion of chance entered

---

[13] This part is based on Peter Wiedemann's ideas that were originally applied to environmental risk-assessment Wiedemann, P. (1992). Taboo, sin, risk. Changes in the Social Perception of Hazards. In: *Risk is a construct*. Berlin & Knesebeck.

Fig. 3.1 Interaction between taboo, sin and risk "filters" of sexuality (taken from Bianchi (2020), inspired by Wiedemann (1992))

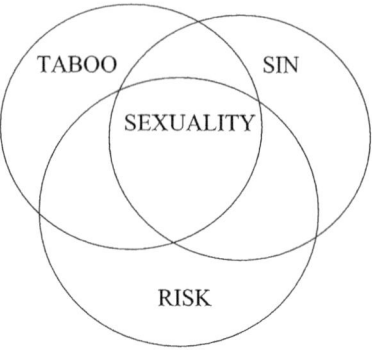

human discourse: *How likely is that a fatal plane/car/train crash will occur? How likely am I to catch HIV during a single unprotected act of sexual intercourse? What is the likelihood of my becoming pregnant using different forms of contraception?*

Thus far, each of these three concepts has more or less functioned within its "typical historical period." The problem arises when we realize that all three concepts—taboo, sin and risk—and the associated cognitive mechanism (animist, deist/analogical or causal/probabilistic), as well as the mutually conflicting distribution of authority and responsibility for negative phenomena among social actors, are still used simultaneously in contemporary discussions on sexuality within a single culture (see Fig. 3.1). In the same family it may be *taboo* to walk around the house naked, *a sin* for either parent to be sexually unfaithful and *a risk* for the teenage children to have unprotected sex. How can we achieve consistent sexual subjectivity when there are three completely contradictory epistemological/cognitive mechanisms regulating different aspects of sexuality? That is a challenge for everyone!

On the one hand there is the cognitive apparatus that determines epistemological practice, while on the other hand there is the narrative understanding of experiences and behaviours, motives, arguments, reasons and justifications of sexual subjectivity. Stories (narratives)—whether our own or reproduced from other people's lives or the media—are central to sexual subjectivity and used in the models that we use when thinking about our own life scenarios, including sexual scenarios, and when making decisions about our future. In an earlier study involving various research methods (qualitative and quantitative), we (Popper et al., 1997) identified four types of justification used to explain undesirable sexual behaviours (Frame 3.4):

1. Low (poor) social and emotional quality of the childhood home environment
2. Disappointment, disenchantment at breaking up with one's true love
3. Serial monogamy
4. Pressure to have sexual intercourse

Frame 3.4   Four Types of Justification Narratives for Explaining Undesirable Sexual Behaviour:

1. *Low (poor) social and emotional quality of the childhood home environment* refers mainly to a cold emotional atmosphere in the family, where there is no open expression of love and acceptance, and there is a disproportionate amount of physical and mental punishment. Children who grow up in this type of environment long for acceptance and love, and in puberty begin seeking these among their peers. They have never learnt to express them themselves and have no knowledge of the mechanisms for gradually building and maintaining a relationship. They may therefore resort to the simple mechanism of "buying" attention and sexual passion in exchange for their own sexual attraction and co-operation. As they have not learnt to give or receive love, a relationship based on sexual satisfaction (mainly regarding the other) quickly falls apart. They are almost guaranteed to seek another partner using a similar scenario.

2. *Disappointment at breaking up with their true love* may trigger risky sexual scenarios in young adults, and frequently in girls who have grown up in a psychologically satisfactory, but often excessively protective, family atmosphere. A cossetted child is one brought up to live in an idealistic world filled with love. At a certain age, they will find a partner they have high and often unrealistic expectations of and want to spend the rest of their life with. The difference between the ideal and the reality begins to emerge sooner or later, and the partnership may come to an end. They will be disappointed, lack the appropriate coping skills, and may opt for a simple compensatory mechanism to regain their lost self-respect and self-confidence by finding a "quick" superficial sexual relationship or indeed relationships. Motivation may

(continued)

Frame 3.4   continued

include revenge—towards their previous partner, but also towards those who fall in love with them and whom they manipulate.

3. *Serial monogamy* "enjoys" a relatively high level of moral acceptance in Slovakia. Generally, there is far greater tolerance of someone having a series of sexual partners, but never more than one at a time, than there is of someone who has only ever had two partners, but simultaneously (e.g. when married). Public opinion seems unwilling to recognize the risks of serial monogamy—especially the risk of sexually transmitted diseases. As all relationships, even short-lived ones, go through a period of infatuation and hence mutual trust (often irrational), the couple feel safe. This is the source of negative attitudes to the use of condoms, which are associated with random, one-off sex with a random partner.

4. *Pressure to have sexual intercourse* may be direct (overt) or indirect (covert). Overt pressure tends to be found in existing partner relationships and is used most by men as a form of emotional blackmail. The mechanism of covert pressure is most frequently found among young sexually inexperienced people who feel like outsiders when tales of real or invented sexual experiences are told in their peer groups. In an attempt to maintain their group identity, they may come under pressure to have any kind of sex—a one-night stand, random sex—with any willing partner and without being aware of the potential risks.

3.3.5   Roots of Violent Sexual Subjectivity: The Subjectivity of the Boundary Between Wanted and Unwanted Sex and Sexuality in the Media

Another important aspect of sexual subjectivity is the roots of violent/ unwanted sexual acts. It may concern capturing the *intersubjectivity* of the sex actors, but it may also concern disclosing the position in which sexuality is presented in the media—in the context of politics and violence. Obtaining knowledge about both these aspects (intersubjectivity and the media) requires us to build on the same textual epistemology but using a fundamentally different methodology—the first requires interpretative approaches and discourse analysis, the second one benefits from, e.g. sophisticated mathematical-probabilistic tools for analysing texts.

Concerning the intersubjectivity of sexual actors, an important source of violent sexual subjectivity can be located in the *inconsistence* and *incongruence* of sexual scripts (Bianchi & Reháková, 2013; Bianchi & Fuskova, 2018; see also Bianchi, 2020). Sexual scripts (Simon, 1996) serve to guide sexual interaction between subjects. There are several levels of script that actors can use, each of them drawing on different syntaxes: the cultural/socio-normative syntax, peer-syntax, interpersonal/dyadic and intrapsychic (Simon, 1996; Bianchi & Fuskova, 2018). In my previous research (Bianchi & Reháková, 2013) we identified a significant reduction in the proportion of dyadic and intrapsychic syntax and increase in cultural syntax in the sexual scripting of marginalized girls from socially disadvantaged environment who were under 15 when they had their sexual debut and became a mother at around that age. Drawing on Simon (1996), this indicates that, in these young women, master paradigms have a strong influence on sexual scripting via obedience to cultural patterns (male vs female sexual roles)—in contrast to the majority population where we observed predominantly post-paradigmatic sexual scripting in which interactive/dyadic intrapsychic syntaxes were strongly represented. In terms of discourse, the specific textuality of these four syntaxes and the tectonics (and how these interact, see Curt, 1994) need to be taken into account when considering how these determine sexual subjectivity. Our study (Bianchi & Fuskova, 2018, see also Bianchi, 2020) showed that we can question the assumption that sexual subjects have a (mental) boundary between wanted and unwanted in sexual interaction, especially young males. The participants talked only experientially of "something like a boundary," "during the ride," mainly by trying out whatever the partner agrees to, whereas young women may have pre-existing limits on their expectations of sexual interaction based on either religious norms or parental expectations. The study, however, can be interpreted as indicating that value inconsistencies between a person's syntaxes or the value incongruence of a syntax between two actors may cause disagreement—if unnegotiated—and undermine the sexual subjectivity of the "weaker" partner. However, this hypothesis needs further research.

Negative aspects of sexual subjectivity may be constructed not just in the interaction between sexual actors but by the media as well. Another study (Bianchi & Fuskova, 2015) shows that over a seven-year period

(2005–2006 vs 2012–2013) there has been a shift away from highlighting and tackling sexual violence against women towards sexual violence to children. There was noticeably more sexualization in the press than on television, in commercial media than in public service media and in tabloids than in serious newspapers. The political aspects of sexuality, erotica and intimacy, however, were covered mainly by public service media and serious newspapers. The coverage of violence and sexuality, and erotica and intimacy, related mainly to children, and in the case of television in recent years at least the social focus has shifted from women to children. Moreover, there has been a large increase in the overall number of items about violence. Thus we could produce strong evidence of a significant divide between, on the one hand, the public service and quality press commercial media, which "cover" the political aspects of sexuality (addressing issues of responsibility, ethics and prevention as well), and, on the other hand, the tabloid media, which lead in reporting sexuality-violence (Bianchi & Fuskova, 2015). The tabloids clearly have a potentially negative effect on sexual subjectivity bearing in mind the power of discourse as social practice (Stainton Rogers, 2003) and the psychological effects of discourse highlighted by Carla Willig, mainly its effect on people's actions, positioning and subjectivity (Willig, 2003).

What stands out the most though is the exposure of intimacy and sexuality, which can be considered to be a reflection of a relatively strong attack on sexual norms in particular. The large number of media items dedicated to revealing sexuality in all its various forms is a sign that the norm transgression is consensual and hence more about a change or a shift in social norms (determining sexual subjectivity) and not just the sporadic violation of sexual norms in the media. This observation resonates with the intimate citizenship thesis highlighted by Ken Plummer (2003) and the call for the transformation versus transmutation of intimacy (cf. Bianchi, 2010a, b, c, 2020), but it also points to the need for a broader discussion on what it means for the subject to be both intimate and public, as raised recently by Georges Teyssot (see Teyssot, 2010) in the context of the media. Teyssot elaborates on the intimacy–extimacy[14] dualism originally proposed and developed by Jacques Lacan. Teyssot offers a historical overview of the divide-approaching-and-merging between the private and the public, resulting in their current apparent (con)fusion via the internet where all media are present and via social networks in particular.

---

[14] More on the intimacy–extimacy dualism in Chap. 4.

The Lacanian intimacy–extimacy dialectics was also utilized in a modi-fied way by Serge Tisseron (2002, 2011). Tisseron highlights two facts that are relevant to the discussion about media and intimacy: (1) the con-tent of the intimacy is not necessarily fully accessible even to the subject:

> Mais l'intimité comporte aussi une autre dimension: ce que chacun ignore sur lui-même. (Tisseron, 2002)
> [However, there is another dimension to intimacy: that which we do not know about ourselves].

Thus, the media may "prompt" the intimate subject and substitute the contents we are unaware of with banal phrases.

More importantly, Tisseron (2011) stresses (2) that there is a process of "controlled" opening and testing of the intimate contents of the subject by the process of extimacy—by opening and offering it to other eyes or to the public, a sort of "confirmation/testing of the intimate through "the other." Tisseron points out that extimacy is—due to its active and selective nature—distinct from exhibitionism and conformism:

> Nous avons proposé en 2001 le mot «extimité» pour rendre compte de cette dynamique. Nous le devons à J. Lacan, qui l'avait proposé pour illustrer le fait que rien n'est jamais ni public ni intime, dans la logique de la figure mathématique appelée «bande de Moebius», pour laquelle n'existe ni «dehors» ni «dedans». Nous avons repris le mot en lui donnant une signifi-cation différente: il est pour nous le processus par lequel des fragments du soi intime sont proposés au regard d'autrui afin d'être validés. Il ne s'agit donc pas d'exhibitionnisme. L'exhibitionniste est un cabotin répétitif qui se complaît dans un rituel figé. Au contraire, le désir d'extimité est inséparable du désir de se rencontrer soi-même à travers l'autre et d'une prise de risques. (Tisseron, 2011)

Extimacy, as defined above, definitely requires a good emotional condi-tion of the subject in order to dare the risks involved, requires courage and social skills and can bring satisfaction through the authentication of the subject but it can also harm the subject if the intimacy juxtaposed with the external environment (including all media content) is rejected or if the subject encounters obstacles. Performed extimacy can therefore be seen as a good indicator of the maturity of the human subject.

SUMMARY

In this chapter I have attempted to illustrate the importance of the subjective dimension of sexuality, despite it being mainly socially and culturally rooted. It is not just that a person's sexuality is played out in their head but also that the subjective meanings of sexuality (and its limits to violence) in our heads are to a great extent social and cultural products that are formed within language. This illustration of the interindividual, group and cross-cultural diversity in what sex and sexual satisfaction mean to people and in the motives for having sex could serve as inspiration when designing more effective sex education and sexual health promotion campaigns.

CHAPTER 4

Collective Subjectivity—Intimacy, Norms, Gender and Intimate Citizenship

Abstract This chapter looks at collective subjectivity—the level of subjectivity at which people act primarily as "group members" with various types of shared identity. It can be illustrated by looking at intimacy (its transmutation from intimacy in relationships and intimacy through individual identity; and its extimacy) and gender identity. And by thinking about new normative trends in society and in ethics before ending with a conceptualization of intimate citizenship that links sexuality and intimacy to citizenship and politics.

4.1 THE INTIMACY–EXTIMACY DIALECTICS OF TRANSMUTED INTIMACY

In Sect. 3.3.5 I briefly introduced an inspirational approach to the dynamic interaction between the intimate aspects of the subject and how these relate to the external arena. In juxtaposition to the historical, literary and artistic interest in human intimacy—the feeling of being close and open towards someone else—scientists have shown an interest in extimacy. This concept was first presented by Jacques Lacan in his 1969 lectures—as Serge Tisseron recalls: he "had proposed it to illustrate the fact that nothing is ever neither public nor intimate, in the logic of the mathematical figure called 'Moebius strip', for which there is neither 'outside' nor 'inside'" (Tisseron, 2011, [translated from French by the author]). Tisseron adopted a more active approach and used the meaning of extimacy to capture the active process of the subject. When we talk about an intimate partner with our friends or parents, we extimate our intimate relationship and accept the risk of being either accepted or rejected. We may experiment with alternations of extimacy towards various recipients and social environments and monitor diverse feedback. Kissing on public transport is a similar test—couples test out both their intimate relationship and the social norm. If our partner is of the same sex, in a homophobic environment the risk of rejection is higher than the likelihood of the extimacy being accepted. Extimacy is, thus, a good indicator of the subject's psychological maturity—the willingness to take risks and the capacity to cope with the risk whilst obtaining support/confirmation of our intimate "world."

When thinking about the intimacy–extimacy dialectics within the psychological subject, the ontology of intimacy may be important. What do we mean by intimacy? In previous work (Bianchi, 2010a, 2020) I introduced the transmutation of intimacy, suggesting that both the substance and nature of intimacy is changing. The 30 years of discussion on the changing types of intimacy is best captured in the work of Anthony Giddens and Lynn Jamieson; nonetheless the very substance of intimacy requires elaboration.

Whereas in psychology, the first functional plane of intimacy is satisfying human needs (cf. Erikson, 1968; Prager, 1995; Kelly, 2007), in sociology a series of arguments has drawn attention to the dramatic turn in intimacy (cf. Luhmann, 1986; Sennett, 1986; Bauman, 2003, Maffesoli, 1985/1993, 2012, 2014). Consequently intimacy has now become the source of a person's identity in society—regardless of whether that society is labelled late-modern, postmodern, the information society, global society or multicultural society.

Michel Maffesoli, despite intimacy not explicitly being his primary focus, supports the idea that intimacy has been substituted by identity. On the one hand he highlights the growing pursuit of "togetherness without finality – being together to 'be together', not to 'reach something'. But he also reminds us of the radicalization (going back to its roots) in preferences for sensuality and emotionality in social merging and in replacing 'cogito ergo sum' with 'I am because others think of me'" (Maffesoli,

1985/1993, 2012, 2014). This last symptom of the transformation of society today is a good indicator of the shift from intimacy satisfaction via the emphasis on shared goals (and commitments) with others to intimacy satisfaction via the emphasis on identity (being perceived by others). The most marked examples here are the processes associated with Facebook, Instagram and similar social platforms, whereby individuals attain "intimacy satisfaction" from being perceived by others (resulting in an apparent identity), but with no intimacy commitment.[1] If we return to the beginning of this chapter—to the concept of extimacy—what action would we perform to perform extimacy of this kind of transmuted intimacy? Take a selfie and post it on Instagram: I extimate my body, my appearance, my mood and my style in the picture, I risk rejection but I expect to be confirmed and rewarded by numerous "likes."

[1] Support for this thesis can be found in the work of Byung Chul Han (2012/2016):

...today is undergoing something that ruins love much more than the infinite freedom [of choice] and unlimited possibilities. The crisis of love is amplified not only by increased supply of other "others", but also by the erosion of "the other" ... walking hand in hand with the gradual narcissification of the self. We live in a society that is becoming increasingly narcissistic. Libido gets invested primarily into our own subjectivity. (pp. 208-209) [translated from Czech by the author]

and Z. Bauman:

In our world of rampant 'individualization' relationships are mixed blessings. They vacillate between sweet dream and a nightmare, and there is no telling when one turns into the other. Most of the time the two avatars cohabit – though at different levels of consciousness. In a liquid modern setting of life, *relationships are perhaps the most common, acute, deeply felt and troublesome incarnations of ambivalence.* (Bauman, 2003, p. VIII, emphasis added)

In a consumer culture like ours, which favours products ready for instant use, quick fixes, instantaneous satisfaction, results calling for no protracted effort, foolproof recipes, all-risk insurance and money-back guarantees relationships are hard to form. (Bauman, 2003, p. 7)

4.2   New Kinds of Moral Norms and New Sexual Subjectivities

The great variety in meanings of sex—whether among the heterosexual or homosexual population, young or old—clearly reflects what William Simon was getting at with his three types of sexual script syntax—intrapsychic, interpersonal/dyadic and cultural/societal (Simon, 1996). In our study exploring the boundary between wanted and unwanted sex (Bianchi & Fúsková, 2018) we suggested a fourth syntax—peer-syntax. Discursively, the tectonics of these four syntaxes may prove useful to those who decide to dig deeper into the determinants of our sexual subjectivity, which has become unmoored from the traditional arena of dichotomies (good–bad, male–female, hetero–homo, married–sinful, etc.). The plurality (and diversity) of these sources and experiences is most important when considering sexual subjectivity. The more varied the resources, the more diverse the figurative forms of sexual subjectivity.

Today's world is a far cry from the times of Immanuel Kant, when moral essence was an immanent attribute of the individual and there was minimal variety, except for doing good or bad according to universal criteria. As illustrated by Anthony Giddens' (1992) assertion that people need to explore themselves, their narratives of self and constructions of self, and in so doing create their own moral constructions. Plummer refers to Starker (1989) when he points out that: "In the early 1970s, sexual self-help books were a leading nonfiction category, a reflection and reinforcement of the dramatic liberalization in moral standards and the modification of social values" (Plummer, 1995: 99). The idea that morality is individually constructed negates universal morality. An individual moral construction (regardless of the extent to which it encompasses any of the big traditional ethical systems) is a *contradictio in adjecto*.[2]

So do we live in an era of moral neutrality (or a moral vacuum) as Sarah Crompton points out in relation to some current art/film streams (Crompton, 2002)? Or is the current era generating alternative moral criteria and procedures to substitute the fading universal morality?

The pragmatist tradition holds that we need to hear new stories and anticipate how they might change our lives when we do. Plummer draws on Richard Rorty (1989) when he claims that "human suffering can only

---

[2] Anthony Giddens (1992) talked of the apparent oxymoron of the *need for moral self-construction*.

be reduced through an improved sensitivity to the voices of the suffering, and this is a matter of detailed description" (Plummer, 1995: 166). This (bottom-up) process of generating narratives of self is now in part the task of much of popular culture, and it therefore cannot be easily dismissed. Rorty opined that "the novel, the movie and the TV programme have, gradually but steadily, replaced the sermon and the treatise as the principal vehicles of moral change and progress," thus opening a new arena for a "substitute" for the fading universal morality. At that time Rorty could not of course include future "vehicles" in his list of the new normative processes—the internet and the (new) social media. Nonetheless it seems that the almost complete openness and universal accessibility of the internet renders it a means of "absolute direct democracy," as well as the ultimate perfect tool for manipulating and exploiting public opinion and the subject. "The sexual revolution has brought greater autonomy, openness, democratic intimacies, broader citizenship on one side against unease, uncertainty, pain and anguish on the other. Greater sexual freedom has brought immense gains but it has its costs" (Weeks, 2007, p.136). The highest price of this freedom is the loss of an order and/or the compulsion to seek out a new social order or rather new social orders.

It is this neuralgic point—the lack of positive support for moral "decision-making" of the subject, so fundamentally different to the great moral narratives of the past with their moral imperatives and incentives—that some current thinkers have sought to resolve: Rosi Braidotti (2009), Carol Gilligan (1982) and Michel Maffesoli (2006). All these efforts concern the interaction and clash or discursive tectonics—to use Beryl Curt's terminology (1994)—between the two opposing trends: on the one hand the progressive liberalization of norms and deconstruction of traditional concepts around intimacy, sexuality and reproduction (emerging "new" intimacies, "new" sexualities, polyamory [consensual non-monogamy], asexualities, fluid and non-binary sexual identities, any queer sexuality, assisted reproduction, surrogate motherhood and non-traditional forms of parenthood), and on the other hand the consequences of the *post-secular turn*[3] (the risks of which are most evident in the attack on gender

---

[3] The post-secular turn can be briefly characterized as the "second gasp" of conservative Christian ideologies and institutions in the last 20 years, which liberated it from the need to defend ontological questions (no longer relevant because of the distancing effect of the post-Nietzschean death of metaphysics), and which are successfully countering the modern achievements of secular liberalism in the second half of the twentieth century (see, e.g. Vattimo, 2002; Rorty and Vattimo, 2007; Caputo and Vattimo, 2007).

equality, the favouring of mothers over women, the subjugation of women's rights to those of the embryo and child, the dividing line between LGBT individuals and the essence of humanity and dismissal of their right to have rights, the demonization of all forms of homosexuality and transsexuality and the "demolition" of sexuality by reproduction, linked to campaigns against contraception, family planning and extra-marital sex, the call for sexual abstinence to solve the HIV epidemic and systematic attacks on biogenetics [genetic technologies] and the theory of evolution).

Braidotti (2009, p.46) asserts that we need to replace negative ethics with a **positive (affirmative) ethics** that prioritizes *ethical relationships over the moral essence of the social subject*. The emphasis on relatedness expresses "a pragmatic approach that defines ethics as a practice that cultivates positive (affirmative) modes of relation, active forces, and values." In contrast to traditional morality, the implementation of established protocols and rules and ethical relationships could create new forms of the world by mobilizing resources such as our desires and imaginations. These driving forces concretize in social and material relationships and form an interlinking network. This vision of ethics is not restricted to ethical thinking on the most diverse kinds of human otherness but opens it up to non-human (sub-human), post-human and inhuman subjects. The inclusion of non-human (sub-human) ethical relationships is key to an ecophilosophy that is not aimed merely at the biological substrate but should be understood as a nature–culture continuum in which subjects construct their own multidimensional relationships. These of course include cultural diversity and social sustainability. Braidotti (2009, p. 47) has stressed the "need to create the conditions for the emergence of affirmative relations, by cultivating relational ethics of becoming. [...] The other is a threshold of transformative encounters. [...] The 'difference' expressed by subjects especially positioned as 'other-than' [...] has a potential for transformative or creative becoming. The 'difference' is not an essential given, but a project and a process that is ethically coded." For Braidotti (2009, p. 47), this post-secular feminist ethics involves three major shifts: (1) from Kantian universal morality to a radical ethics of transformation, (2) from a unitary rationality-driven consciousness to an ontology aimed at the visions of subjectivity propelled by affects and relations, (3) from a subjectivity positioned as the negation of others (me = not them) to self-affirmation of the subjectivity of positive (affirmative) reciprocity as a process of self-creation. Aiming at her sceptics, Braidotti added: "Far from falling into moral relativism, this [ethics] results in a proliferation of locally situated micro-universalist claims" (Braidotti, 2009; p. 49).

Braidotti (2009), having sketched out her ethical "solution," turns, finally, to affect. She argues that a positive (affirmative) ethics should lead to the transmutation of values—changing their nature towards "sensitive" issues. She suggests that the systematic turn in ethics will change things so that *the distinction will no longer be between good and bad, but between affirmation and negation instead,* and so ultimately between a positive and negative affect (as the quality and setting of basic public discourses). How might this impact on, e.g. sexual discourses? Homosexuality might cease to be seen as "bad" by those who disagree with it; they will merely need to reject it and that should satisfy them. At the same time, for its supporters, homosexuality will no longer be aimed at a "good" thing; they will merely need to accept it.

In recent years, Carol Gilligan's (1982) approach—**the ethics of care**—has been applied to various social practice contexts—medical and patient care or social work, in relation to wide-ranging aspects of sexuality or sex education, or the needs of sex offenders or sexual minorities (cf. Bosá, 2017; Ward & Salmon, 2011). It is a normative ethical approach that has developed out of feminism. In contrast to consequentialist and deonto-logical ethical theories which emphasize generalizable standards and impartiality, the ethics of care emphasizes the importance of how we approach (diverse) individuals/subjects. The distinction can be seen in various moral questions: "What is just?" versus "How should we respond?". Gilligan has criticized the application of generalized standards on the grounds that it is morally problematic, since moral blindness or indiffer-ence may arise. The moral "imperative" in the ethics of care can be formu-lated as the need to respond to the various needs of diverse individuals/subjects.

Whether and which of these (Braidotti, Gilligan) or any other approach to creating a new ethical paradigm will succeed in becoming a broadly distributed and accepted mechanism for enabling moral decisions is an open question. It is, however, a fact, that in order to succeed, it would have to "win" the "discursive tectonics battle" over the spontaneous social process that is ongoing in Western society and which Michel Maffesoli expressed thus: "Ethics of postmodernity is the ethics of the aesthetic. The shadow of Dionysus is floating over the postmodern societies" (Maffesoli, 2006, p. 140). In other words, the new ethical paradigm would have to prevail over the super-egoist-narcissistic and socially blind thinking of the subject: "What I like is morally ok."

Bearing that last sentence in mind, we simply have to nod our heads when looking at how sexual subjectivities have evolved recently. The emergence of complex conceptualizations of LGBT+, polyamory/consensual non-monogamy and asexuality, along with sexual non-binarity and fluidity corresponds perfectly with this cultural phenomenon of identity narcissism. It follows calls for political, societal, cultural and normative acknowledgement of the multiplicity of diverse sexual subjectivities that are invisible, repressed or substituted, and treated under different "labels." For example Justin Mogilski (2021) defends an evolutionary explanation of polyamory as an alternative to infidelity, in which both performed patterns are thought to be driven by an urge to satisfy the need for sexual diversity.

4.3   Current Regional "Narratives"
of Gender Subjectivity

This mosaic of subjectivities includes the emergence of gender identity. In this chapter I do not intend to repeat the history of gender awareness in psychology or summarize the importance of gender and social class in critical social science and psychology in particular (cf. Walkerdine, 1996, 2002; Hallway, 1998). Instead I will illustrate the difficulties of establishing gender subjectivity by presenting recent findings from Slovakia—indicative of the Central European realm of post-socialist civilization at the turn of the centuries. The findings were obtained from several international and national research projects and reveal interesting aspects of gender subjectivity.

In projects addressing **European, national, regional and personal identity** I and my team have spent several years exploring the interdependencies between these distinct levels of identity. The most significant sources of young people's identity were their family and friends, followed by education and career/profession. Regional, national, and European belonging saturated their personal identity far less, and **sex and gender the least**. Comparative analyses have shown that young people in Bratislava and Prague consistently have the highest levels of gender-stereotyping along with the lowest interest in gender-related issues when compared with samples from other European cities and/or regions—Edinburgh,

Manchester, Madrid, Bilbao, Bielefeld, Chemnitz, the Bregenz area of Vorarlberg and Vienna (Bianchi & Lášticová, 2004, 2005; Bianchi et al., 2007). Nonetheless, young women identified more with the European Union than young men did. This may be linked to the influence of gender-equity influence (through EU policies), which is targeted more strongly at women than men.

Further examples of exploring the collective regional narratives on gender subjectivity draw on sexuality and sexual victimization. In our project exploring **constructions of masculinity and femininity in relation to future romantic partnerships** (Popper et al., 2006), we focused on the proportion of gender stereotypes. Specifically, this meant the role played by contrasting qualities typically found in male/female gender stereotypes (rationality/emotionality and dominance/submission) in young people's expectations. The analysis of the narratives the participants constructed in focus groups showed that: (1) rationality and dominance attributes determine the romantic relationship—independently of whether they are held by a man or woman, (2) dominance gives the bearer greater agency in influencing the relationship, (3) people with a "full" gender stereotype profile (dominant+rational, or submissive+emotional) are easier to deal with than those with a combined profile (e.g. dominant+emotional, submissive+rational) and (4) female participants' preferred male characteristics were—certain decisiveness/dominance+flexibility/capacity to adjust to partner and situation+no violence (zero tolerance of male violence).

In another study (Bianchi et al., 2002) we found that the **subjective constructions of sex (sexual intercourse) and gender (different types of masculinity and femininity) were interconnected to the extent that these two processes can be considered inseparable**; the acquisition of a certain gender construction (e.g. liberal or traditional) has at least an implicit meaning in (current or future) understandings of sex(uality). These processes are, moreover, directly linked to the degree of health risk-taking during sexual interactions and the risk of yielding to pressure or frustration associated with gender stereotypes in sexual interactions.

An international comparative study on sexual victimization (Krahé et al., 2015) found **a paradoxical distribution of reported sexual victimization in males and females**. Surprisingly, in some European cultures, males reported a higher incidence of sexual victimization than females. On average around one-third of respondents (aged 18–27) reported experiencing unwanted sexual activity. The overall frequency of reporting was significantly higher in women, but in several countries

(Greece, Cyprus, Lithuania) the male/female ratio was inverted. In order to explain this paradox we conducted a qualitative study (Krahé et al., 2016). The questionnaire items measuring sexual victimization were subjected to a post hoc qualitative analysis to determine how participants in particular countries/cultures understood the concepts used in the questions. Although the analysis did not reveal any important gender or country differences in participant understanding of the meaning of sexually relevant concepts (*touching, attempted sexual intercourse, sexual intercourse, use of physical power, taking advantage of the situation, one's authority and verbal pressure*), it explained why men in some countries report experiencing unwanted sexual activity more frequently than women do. In the three countries concerned women have become more assertive in recent years and this may be perceived by men as a threat to their masculine sexual subjectivity. The participants reported potentially feeling victimized as they can see that women are prepared to be more active in initiating sexual contact. This explanation is supported by our previous findings (Krahé et al., 2015) that male victimization correlates negatively with male sexual assertiveness towards women and that male victimization correlates negatively with the gender equity index of the country. There is, evidently, an interaction and habituation effect in place—men find the increase/change in female emancipation frightening—not the high status of gender equity per se. Further research in this area is needed.

Last but not least, I would like to mention an early **cross-cultural study of gender differences between Japan, Sweden and Slovakia in what could be called the** *subjectivity of life-and-death.* The research concerned attitudes, beliefs and opinions about suicide (Eisler et al., 1999). The motivation behind this study was the obvious differences in the culture and value structure between the countries (collectivist, individualist and post-totalitarian pseudo-collectivist). Suicide has different historically determined symbolic meanings in these three countries—for the observer as well as for the actor, i.e. the subject. In Japan, building on the Samurai ethic, committing suicide has never been considered shameful, but rather a premeditated moral action augmenting the subjectivity of the actor. In Sweden where the culture is individualistic and egalitarian and where there is weak social stratification, suicide can be seen as the individual's decision understood through the prism of human nature and individual competitiveness, detached from ethical judgement and, thus, more of a positive than negative aspect of the subject. In Slovakia with its strong Catholic tradition and 40 years of totalitarian communist ideology, suicide is a sin and, moreover, the subject's failure to adjust to the public arena where everyone was expected to be happy in socialist "heaven." The main questions in the study were: (1) Are attitudes, beliefs and opinions on suicide most positive in Japan and most negative in Slovakia? and (2) What are the gender differences in these variables? In the quantitative research we used Lester and Bean's (1992) questionnaire, "Attitudes, beliefs and opinions about suicide." Based on a MANOVA analysis with country (3) x gender (2), both country and gender were shown to have a main effect in most of the scales—attitudes, beliefs and opinions about suicide were most positive in Japan and most negative in Slovakia. What was surprising though was the gender divide that was manifested in Japan and in Slovakia, and was absent in Sweden. The gender equity that is deeply rooted in Sweden is also manifest in such a sensitive area as suicide. In contrast to Sweden, in Japan and in Slovakia attitudes, beliefs and opinions on suicide in women were significantly more negative than in men.

4.4   PARTICULARIZATION OF THE SUBJECT
AND THE POLITICAL RISKS

In the sociological literature there is increasing promotion of approaches designed to draw attention to the "new" aspects of citizenship—*sexual citizenship* (D.T. Evans, 1993), *intimate citizenship* (Plummer, 1995, 2003) and *cultural citizenship* (Turner, 2001). I have presented and analysed these in detail elsewhere (Bianchi, 2010a, 2020; Bianchi & Luha, 2010) and so here I shall merely highlight the fact that they are all designed to overcome the limits of Marshall's (1950) concept of citizenship based on three categories of rights—civil, political and social rights.[4]

Let's have a closer look at Ken Plummer's concept of intimate citizenship that is aimed at solving the problematic public–private divide and is thus relevant to our discussion of human subjectivity. Intimate citizenship concerns "control (or not) over one's body, feelings, relationships; access (or not) to representations, relationships, public spaces, etc; and socially

---

[4] In rights theories, there are various opinions on how human rights should be categorized. The first generation was concerned with civil and political rights, the second with economic, social, and cultural rights, and the third generation with collective rights relating to the global problems of humankind (for more, see, e.g. Jankuv, 2006). The legal system and human rights is beyond the topic of this book and considered here only in relation to sexuality and intimacy.

grounded choices (or not) about identities, gender experiences, erotic experiences" (Plummer, 1995, p. 151). In other words, intimate citizenship should guarantee the fulfilment of our diversified subjectivity: fulfilling our needs regarding our bodies, feelings and relationships and having guaranteed access to public resources and making decisions regarding our identity, gender, erotic feelings and experiences.

Moreover, the subject is currently under certain pressure from the society (mainly via social media) to showcase his/her specific subjectivities, while society is being transformed into a multi-minority conglomerate where everyone is striving for acknowledgement of their uniqueness and demands for public resources and spaces for fulfilment. Numerous sub-populations are emerging with specific combinations or mixtures of lifestyle requirements who consequently adopt a particular stance on intimate citizenship, such as people with disabilities or people who are chronically ill, people with specific dietary requirements, public figures, young people, elderly people, ethnic minorities, faith proponents, fluid sexual identity and asexual exponents and many others.

At this point Fukuyama (2018) issues a warning:

> Individuals come to believe that they have a true or authentic identity hiding within themselves that is somehow at odds with the role they are assigned by their surrounding society. The modern concept of identity places a supreme value on authenticity, on the validation of that inner being that is not being allowed to express itself. It is on the side of the inner and not the outer self. Oftentimes an individual may not understand who that inner self really is, but has only the vague feeling that he or she is being forced to live a lie. This can lead to an obsessive focus on the question "Who am I, really?" The search for an answer produces feelings of alienation and anxiety and can only be relieved when one accepts that inner self and receives public recognition for it. And if that outer society is going to properly recognize the inner self, one has to imagine society itself being able to change in fundamental ways. (ibid, p. 54–55)

Paul Reynolds (2010) penned a critical essay exploring the discourses that constitute the basis of the private–public divide (liberalism, conservative values, medical-moral discourse and legal and political regulation). His aim was to highlight the counterproductive nature of this divide, especially where intimacy (with its sensory, emotional and affective phenomenology) is seen as the central concept in the intimate citizenship project "launched" by Ken Plummer (1995), in which intimacy is transformed into "public intimacies." Reynolds used compelling arguments from political philosophy to support his thesis that the focus on the (liberal) private sphere may present a serious obstacle to introducing intimate citizenship into everyday politics.

Fukuyama then explicitly warns us that the emerging demand for the recognition of dignity based on (disadvantaged) minority identity/identities is not only a psychological-sociological-ethnological-linguistic issue, but a realm of politics (Fukuyama, 2018):

> Demand for recognition of one's identity is a master concept that unifies much of what is going on in world politics today. (ibid, p.16)
>
> Universal recognition has been challenged ever since by other partial forms of recognition based on nation, religion, sect, race, ethnicity, or gender, or by individuals wanting to be recognized as superior. The rise of identity politics in modern liberal democracies is one of the chief threats that they face, and unless we can work our way back to more universal understandings of human dignity, we will doom ourselves to continuing conflict. (ibid, p. 17)

Summary

In seeking to improve the sexual and reproductive health and rights of human sexual beings, it is useful to reflect on what is currently happening to our intimacy, gender identity and the norms that "regulate" our expectations of sexuality. The twenty-first century is without doubt a historical period in which sexuality has become a political commodity and in which defending human dignity and sexual well-being is not only a job for psychology and medicine, but requires us to think of sexual subjectivities in their cultural and political dimensions.

CHAPTER 5

Epistemological and Methodological Challenges of Subjectivity

Abstract Some may consider this chapter to be the most daring in the book. In my view it is the trickiest one—at least from my "subjective" point of view. Epistemological and methodological challenges require very broad, deep and integrative insights into the research matter, but must of course be innovative and daring as well. Innovations emerge mostly out of frustration with traditional procedures. That was my main driver: to learn more about sexual subjectivity than can be achieved by assessing quantitative surveys. Hence I became a strong promoter of Q-methodology and its integral application with a discursive asset. Here I present some of the crucial and pioneering applications of Q-methodology in my region that constitute a new epistemological use of the Q paradigm (very different from its original applications by Stephenson, which did not link it to the discursive asset). This chapter also contributes in several ways to the discourse analysis of sexuality issues based on my research (analysis of discursive practice and analysis of discursive resources—with interpretative links to mainstream psychology). In addition, this chapter includes my assessment of epistemological innovations obtained through a series of studies conducted and published by a team led by David Schmitt (International Sexuality Description Project I + II) which I had the honour of being a part of. The epistemological triangulation that was central to the study was broadly overlooked, and it remained in the shadow of raw and extremely interesting quantitative sexuality data measured in the project.

Here I try to shift the focus onto the epistemological innovations of the study, which contribute to the focus on human subjectivity (Readers enthusiastic about epistemology and the mixed-method approach may find the deeply motivated work of Wendy Olsen on *realistic methodology* interesting (Olsen, 2007, 2012; see also Patomäki & Wight, 2000). Building on Bhaskar's Marxist, structuralist and Gandhian *A Realist Theory of Science* (1975) Olsen's aim is to foster a more realist research in social science. Realist methodologists are sceptical of using the nomothetic method (identifying and testing the laws of society). The main methodological innovations that arise from realism are the importance of methodological awareness, leaving hypothesis testing behind, and the centrality of doing retroduction—reasoning about why things happen, including why the data appear the way they do (along with induction—reasoning from data to generality; deduction—reasoning from generality to data via hypothesis testing; abduction—reasoning from immersion in a scene to a verbal summary). The last section in this chapter explores the potential for adopting methodological tools from "other" sciences for use in research on human subjectivity—an integral model of design thinking, system thinking—systems theory and system dynamics modelling.

5.1   Q-Methodology for Studying "Operant Subjectivity"

Besides introducing sexuality as a research topic in the post-totalitarian academia in Slovakia during the early 1990s, I, together with my colleagues, used the opportunity to introduce innovative epistemological and methodological approaches to psychological research. This concerns the use of Q-methodology and various uses for analysing discourse(s). Distant approaches for many perhaps, but surprisingly they share a common purpose and close links.

Q-methodology is a "procedure" described originally by Stephenson in 1953 when interested in the study of human expressivity ("operant subjectivity") based on the analysis of quantitative social-psychological data (see Kerlinger, 1972). The "Q" symbolizes a counterposition to "R," while "R" is the conventional view used in mathematical statistics to analyse relationships among variables. "R" symbolizes the search for relationships among variables—data reduction by identifying variable-relationships. Participants/cases in a sample serve to support the statistical validity of such operations. "R" procedures allow us to compare variables, looking for correlations and the higher-level organization of variables (up to causal relations).

When applying "Q" methodology, the matrix with the variable data from a number of participants is turned 90 degrees, allowing data reduction on the participant side. The aim of any subsequent mathematical procedure is to look for relationships among participants/cases. The result may be, e.g. the factor structure of the cases, where each factor consists of participants with statistically similar feeding into each of the variables. The difference between Q-methodology and R-methodology is that in the latter a set of variables is submitted to a group of people, whereas in Q-methodology a set of people is submitted to a group of variables. Somewhat paradoxically, but logically nonetheless, interest in this method was revived with the introduction of critical psychology and the exploration of the constructivist and discursive language paradigm—the qualitative epistemological arena. Why? And how? When the variables measured in the data collection are statements expressing various opinions (in language) about a certain issue, the factors received via the factor analysis of the participants are composed of people who have significantly similar opinions about that issue but significantly dissimilar ones from all the other participants. Therefore, each of the factors can be understood as an expression of group subjectivity and specific discourse on the issue studied as well. Returning to Stephenson's original motivation: when the items in a Q-methodological study are authentic expressions from ecologically valid discourse(s) on a given issue, we can expect the factor structure to reflect the diversity of operant subjectivity—it will be sufficiently typical of a specific individual construction of understanding human conduct on that given issue.

The re-introduction of Q-methodology[1] aids the constructive critique of psychometrics and traditional empiricist positivism in psychology. Therefore, the introduction of Q-methodology—a mathematical-statistical method—together with discursive epistemology and methodology provide synergy in psychological research and may give psychological research a new quality and contribute significantly to psychological knowledge on human nature.

---

[1] Most recently the Q-approach has been found in current computational instruments, "hiding" behind "latent group analysis"—a subtype of latent profile analysis (Neely-Barnes 2010).

We published our first Q-methodological study integrating the discursive paradigm into this quantitative approach in 1999 in the journal *Československá psychologie* (Bianchi et al., 1999a). It confirmed the interpretative power of Q-methodology within the discursive psychological paradigm. In this study we built on the categorization of four contemporary general discourses on sexuality (as outlined in Sect. 3.2) and searched for a match with nine empirically identified groups/classes of young people. The groups emerged from the Q-analysis following an assessment of various aspects of sexuality expressed in a Q-set of 73 items covering sex activities, partnership, responsibility, faithfulness and risk. With the exception of two groups, the opinions of the remaining seven groups of participants matched various combinations of two general discourses. The opinions of one group of participants corresponded to the Christian-traditional-morals general discourse on sexuality only, while another group's corresponded with the civil liberal general discourse on sexuality only. Moreover, the interpretation of the specific discursive constructions of each virtual Q-sort, i.e. the specific configuration of the 73 items for each group, allowed us to assess the sexual risk-taking aspects of each virtual Q-sort and thus of the participants generating that group. Thus a firm discursive-psychological link to psychological agency was demonstrated.

The study was followed by a comparative one involving participants (aged 16–18 years, N = 188) from three distinct countries/cultures (Catalunia, England, Slovakia) (Stenner et al., 2006). In this collaborative project between the Slovak Academy of Sciences and the British Academy with the participation of the Department of Psychology, University College London, we conducted a study investigating sexual health in young people. The application of Q-methodology in combination with a discursive approach and quantitative analysis enabled the cross-cultural analysis of the subjective understanding of sexual relations (their discursive constructions) and the health implications for young adults. The results showed that diverse understandings of sexual relations differed in the (a) extent of traditionalism versus liberalism, (b) locus of/attribution of responsibility and (c) conceptualization of the love–sex connection.

The evaluation of the empirical material processed using Q-methodology (58 items sorted by 188 participants) yielded several trans-cultural types of sexuality discourse: liberal-hedonistic individualism, liberal orientation to partnerhood with awareness of potential risks, liberal orientation to partnerhood endorsing partnership commitments. Some specific types of sexuality discourse were also identified in specific cultures (countries): liberal orientation to partnerhood relying on "automatic" faithfulness in love (Catalunia), traditional matrimonial relations (Slovakia) and doubting faithfulness as such (Slovakia). Further analysis showed that particular types of discourse differed primarily in two dimensions: in the extent to which they were liberal versus conservative and endorse partnerhood versus individualism. Most of the discursive constructions of sexual relations occurred in all three countries. Some, however, due to cultural incompatibility, emerged in Catalunia and Slovakia but not in England. Obtaining knowledge on the specific constructions of sexual relations has practical implications given the health risks associated with each of them.

Along with this study additional "probes" exploring the integrity of discursive epistemology with the Q-methodology paradigm were conducted under my supervision, published and are open for discussion.[2]

5.2   Q-STUDY AS DISCOURSE ANALYSIS VERSUS "MAINSTREAM" DISCOURSE ANALYSIS

5.2.1   Q-Assisted Discourse Analysis

In Sect. 3.2 I introduced a complex view of a multilevel discursive approach—focusing on sexuality. Discourse analysis is one of the main approaches in the "new" psychology that builds on the epistemological innovations enabled by the twentieth-century linguistic turn in philosophy, sociology and related disciplines. Besides the types of discursive analyses encompassing the analysis of discursive resources (or Foucauldian

---

[2] Červenková, I (2005) Sociálne konštrukcie homosexuality v prostredí školy (*Social constructions of homosexuality in the school environment*). PhD. Thesis, PdF UK, BRATISLAVA, 151 pp., published as: Červenková, I. & Bianchi, G. (2003). Diskurzy homosexuality a vývin sexuálnej identity (*Discourses of homosexuality and the development of sexual identity*). *Československá psychologie*, 47(2), 122–134.
- Fúsková, J. (2016) Reality (de)konštrukcie rodových stereotypov v škole (*Reality of the [de]construction of gender stereotypes at school*). PhD. Thesis. PdF UK, Bratislava, 130 pp.
- Lebedová, I. (2008) Diskurzívne konštrukcie interrupcií u mladých žien – Q-metodologická štúdia (*Discursive constructions of abortions in young women – a Q-methodological study*). Master Thesis, University Prešov., published as: Lebedová, I. & Bianchi, G. (2009). Diskurzívne konštrukcie interrupcií u mladých žien (Q-metodologická štúdia) (*Discursive constructions of abortions in young women – a Q-methodological study*). *Psychológia a patopsychológia dieťaťa*, 44(4), 295–314.

analysis), analysis of discursive practice, critical discourse analysis, conversation analysis, narrative analysis, interpretative phenomenological analysis and so forth, there is, I dare say, a specific form of analysis—the analysis of the discursive nature of the factors (virtual Q-sorts) produced in a Q-analysis (see Sect. 5.1). Following on from the previous section on Q-methodology, here I will briefly remind readers of the close links between Q-methodology and discursive psychology. As mentioned above, virtual Q-sorts resulting from a Q-study represent the structure of the natural discourse of real people, who constitute a particular factor, on a specific issue. The six factors in the Stenner et al. (2006) study represented six such natural discourses. The power of this methodological approach rests in its mathematical capacity, which enables large amounts of discursive data to be easily exploited to identify, e.g. nation-specific discourses on sexuality (the two discourses in Slovakia on traditional matrimonial relations and on doubting faithfulness as such, and one in Catalunia on the liberal approach to partnership dependent on the "automatic" faithfulness of love; all three discourses being significantly distinct from all other discourses and each of them unique for one nationality).

The implementation of this Q-study is a good example of research aimed at, e.g. capturing cultural subjectivity in sexuality.

Besides the implementation of "Q-assisted" discursive analysis the power of the more "traditional" discursive analytical approach (in studying sexuality) is another area I have covered or supervised.

5.2.2   *"Mainstream" Use of Discourse Analysis—Analysis of Discursive Practice*

A good example is Sect. 3.3.1 where I reported on the **subjective meaning of sex in men having sex with men (MSMs)**. That research employed a discourse analysis as well.[3] The study employed the **analysis of discursive practice** (see W. Stainton Rogers, 2003), which enables the researcher to answer questions such as: *What does the person want to achieve in this part of the conversation? How does he/she treat discursive resources?*

The study showed that the degree to which MSMs achieve satisfaction of intimate needs is heavily influenced by societal discrimination. Heteronormative standards frequently affect a wide range of

---

[3] I reported this originally in 2010 (Bianchi, 2010b, c) and the study is fully documented in Bianchi (2020).

conceptualizations of sexuality in MSM and of their meanings of sex, as well as types of coupledom.

5.2.3 "Mainstream" Use of Discourse Analysis—Analysis of Discursive Resources

In a bilateral project between the Institute for Research in Social Communication, Slovak Academy of Sciences, and the Open University, UK, initiated and inspired by Wendy Stainton Rogers, we jointly researched *Sexual Health in Different Multi-Layer Identity Structures* (from cca 1995). The second type of discourse analysis was used here—**the analysis of discursive resources**. It is concerned with how discourses operate as the social and cultural resources people use in their activities and endeavours. Such research attempts to identify and describe the main discourses that play out, how these discourses affect one another, and what identity and agency they provide for their users (Stainton Rogers, 2003, p. 86).

Based on individual semi-structured interviews and focus group discussions we mapped the main **discourses on seduction (and temptation) in Slovakia**. These were then analysed and compared with discourses in England. While temptation is the internal process of considering different alternatives, seduction is an interactive process between the seducer and the seduced within a predominantly sexual–erotic context. The discourses that were identified can be divided into two groups: discourses on vulnerability and discourses on the consequences of surrendering.

There were several *discourses on vulnerability*: (a) biological discourse, justifying surrender in terms of hormones and sexual needs, (b) situational discourse justifying surrender in terms of the availability of the object of temptation, new circumstances, the effect of alcohol and reference-group pressure, (c) discourse on values—people tend to yield to temptation that is not a high priority among their values, (d) discourse on manipulation—open and spontaneous people are more prone to yielding as they are easily influenced and manipulated and (e) therapeutic discourse—people in a state of personal crisis are more prone to endorsing their own value by allowing a prohibited pleasure, e.g. yielding to sexual seduction.

The *discourses on the consequences of surrender* were: (a) the slippery-slope discourse: it is highly probable that surrendering once (e.g. to alcohol) gives rise to repeat surrenders on other things (e.g. sex), (b) discourse on learning: surrendering to temptation can have positive consequences as well—learning and understanding the risks and consequently avoiding having to face similar situations in the future, (c) discourse on moral transformation: experiencing the forbidden stimulates the active deconstruction of ready-made morals and their active transformation into personal (and therefore respected) rules (Bianchi et al., 2005).

In Slovakia, as well in England, we observed (unpublished pilot research) a shift away from the modernist bipolar *good–bad* model—in which people who never surrender were considered to be "saints," moral and strong and those surrendering to temptation were sinners, immoral and weak—to a three-dimensional model. In this model people who never surrender to temptation are considered boring. The third dimension is "autonomous" people who are able to make their own decisions about which temptation to resist and which temptation to indulge in. Those who surrender to all temptations are considered weak (Fig. 5.1).

These preliminary findings are inspirative not just at the theoretical level, but they also may have strong and direct implications for the creation of preventive and health-education messages.

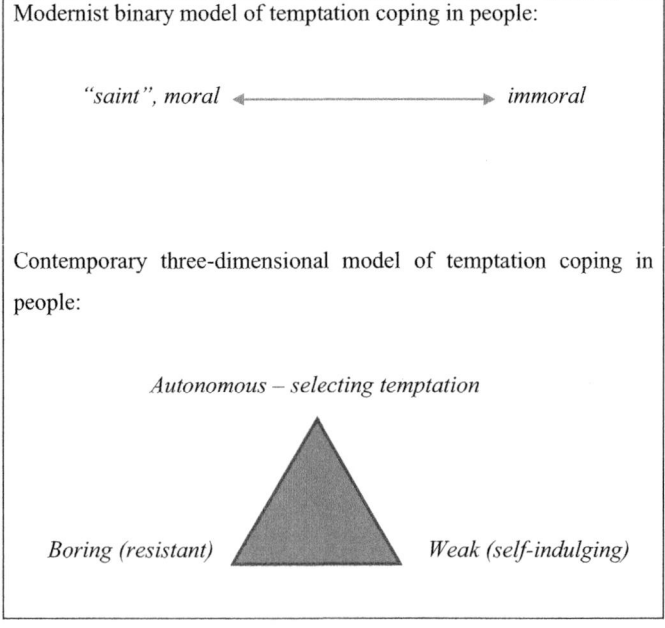

Fig. 5.1   Models of temptation coping

5.2.4 Analysis of Discursive Resources Conductive to Mainstream Psychology (What Are the Minority Discourses on Sexual Seduction[4] in Roma in Slovakia?)

The diversification of discourses on temptation and seduction described above provided the inspiration for conducting a study targeting minority discourses of sexual seduction—seduction discourses among the Roma population in Slovakia (Gondec & Bianchi, 2012).[5] Here I wish to highlight the aspects of the study and the results that contribute to both the discussion on specific (1) **methodological approaches suitable for extracting knowledge on subjectivity**, and to (2) **subjectivity per se**—in this case culturally specific subjectivity in sexual seduction, surrender and resisting or indulging sexual temptation.

The Roma ethnic minority represents a distinct group in Slovakia that differs substantially from the majority population on many indicators. The aim here is not to discuss inclusive, integrationist, assimilationist and segregationist political strategies regarding minority and majority relations. Nonetheless, the reality is that a large section of the Roma population lives in borderline or absolute poverty and this automatically amplifies sexual and reproductive health problems. The ethnological literature deals with the issue of sexual and reproductive health among the Roma in passing

---

[4] In the research on sexuality and sexual health, seduction has received very little systematic attention. Sigmund Freud (1896) was the first to formulate a theory of seduction as a cause of hysteria and obsessive-compulsive disorder resulting from sexual abuse in early childhood. He later abandoned the theory, a move that attracted the criticism of Jean Laplanche (1999), who saw value in the "decentring" effect in Freud's theory, which, unlike later psychoanalytical thinking, did not concentrate solely on the individual and the (ego)centrality of the individual (see also Scarfone, 2001). Seduction is also studied in evolutionary psychology, particularly via the conceptualizing of *mate poaching* (obtaining a sexual partner who is already in a relationship with someone else), which is a key seduction issue relating to partnership-formation strategies. Mate poaching is highly successful (the probability of poaching a partner is more than 75%) and is found in all cultures, with surprisingly few gender differences (Buss, 2006; Schmitt et al., 2004a).

Nonetheless, the psychoanalytical and evolutionary theories do not provide a sufficient basis from which to investigate seduction in terms of its significance to the sexual health of the subject. Seduction was also researched in the 1990s as part of the search for the best preventive strategies to halt the spread of HIV, and in some studies on condom use, but these findings cannot be generalized to the sexual interaction of human subjects in all its complexity (Bird & Harvey, 2000; De Bro et al., 1994; Choi et al., 2004; Kline et al., 1992).

[5] An abridged version of the study was presented recently in Bianchi (2020).

only and contains only secondary sources on seduction. Liégeois (1997: 66) provides some information:

> matrimony is the crucial element of (social) organization, bringing stability but also change. By entering into [a Roma] marriage, the individual takes on the social role of an adult. The bond between two individuals is based on a social agreement between the groups to which they belong.

Bolfíková (2003), in her detailed research on sexual and reproductive health among the Roma people (N = 144; 85% of the sample aged 13–40), documented some of the parameters of sexual and reproductive health that differ substantially from those of the majority population in Slovakia, which when co-occurring present a major source of cumulative risk for the sexual and reproductive health of the Roma.[6]

The aim of this research was to establish which social sources young Roma draw on in forming their ideas about the element of sexual-erotic relations known as seduction. The central questions for the participants were:

1. Could you please tell me a story about seduction? It could be something you've seen on the television, heard, read, or it could be a story from your own personal life.
2. Do these types of things happen to everyone or just some people?

---

[6] For example, one of the strongest predictors of health risks in sexuality, used mainly in international comparisons, is pregnancy rates among women under the age of 20. In Bolfíková's research sample, two thirds of respondents aged 13–15 already had one child. A quarter of female respondents aged 16–20 already had two children, and 6% had three children. These figures differ substantially from the population average: in Slovakia, during the same period, the rate of pregnancy under the age of 20 was 21.8 per thousand women, and eight abortions per thousand women (da Silva, et al., 2011). In the same research 6.94% of respondents had their sexual debut at the age of 13–14 (9.62% of men and 5.43% of women). A relatively high percentage of respondents (11.81%; 15.38% of men and 9.78% of women) were unsure of the year in which they had first had sex. Ideas about what sex would be like were very positive, with 78.86% of respondents considering their prior expectations to be pleasant, nice, happy and good, especially among men (93.31%) and less so among women (72.83%). However, 31.52% of women and 21.15% of men stated that they hadn't known anything about sex before experiencing it. The data show that for most respondents their first sexual contact was unplanned (54.86%; more so among women at 57.61% than among men at 50.00%). More than 17% of respondents stated that they were unaware of any form of contraception. First sexual contact led to pregnancy in 16.67% of cases.

The analysis of the recorded interviews was structured by the modified "analysis of discursive resources" recommended by Willig (1993). The six steps were (where possible) transposed into concepts from mainstream psychology (goals, motivation, vulnerability, responsibility, morality, etc.) in order to be more conductive to the mainstream "reader." To maintain the link with the terminology traditionally used in psychology, we categorized them as follows:[7] Table 5.1:

Table 5.1 Discursive and traditional categories of analysis

Steps of analysis of discursive resources according to Willig— partly modified (Willig, 1993/2013)	Corresponding concepts relevant to mainstream psychology
Discourse characteristics (including the type of setting they sprang from, if they actively reflected cultural specificities or were more universal, how the discourse was valued internally, whether it was a dominant or a minor discourse among the participants)	Would be: "definition"
Constructions of seduction	Would be: "Essence, nature of, morphology,…"
Subjectivity: constructions of subjectivity of the seducer and the seduced; of the man and the woman;	Goals; motivation; vulnerability
Strategies and actions—potential for practical usage—handling the situation;	Tools of seduction; interactions; localization of actions; coping
Subject position towards law, morality	Localization of responsibility
Resources of the discourse	Contexts

The analysis of the 13 interviews yielded six discourses relating to seduction: (1) bonding discourse, (2) consumerist discourse, (3) biological discourse, (4) discourse on the non-existence of seduction/historical seduction, (5) pressure discourse and (6) a discourse on influencing fate. A detailed and structured presentation of these discourses can be found in Bianchi (2020). Here I would like to point out some aspects that illustrate the subjectivity specifics of the Roma discourses on seduction as compared to majority-population discourses on sexual seduction (Bianchi et al., 2005):

---

[7] Not all the categories could be satisfactorily saturated for all the discourses identified; it depended on the depth of the interview and how much was generated. Details are in Table 5.1.

Three of the discourses overlap with the discourses identified within the majority population:

1. The discourse we have called the *biological discourse* here shares discursive elements with the *biological* and *classical gender discourses* identified in Bianchi et al. (2005). Both the *biological discourse* and the *classical gender discourse* share argumentational schemes that refer to a biological predisposition to succumb to the idea that higher levels of activity in sexual-erotic relationships are socially desirable among men. These two discourses construct the man as a "stag" permanently primed for sex and incapable of resisting his biological predispositions.

2. The discourse we referred to as the *consumerist discourse* also appears to be a combination of various discourses. It contains the element of *situatedness* (characterized in Bianchi et al., (2005) as the accessibility of the object of seduction as determined by the new setting, alcohol and pressure from the reference group) as well as general references to *sex-oriented seduction* (as opposed to relationship-oriented) and, particularly when the narrator is a woman, it reveals signs of *gender-stereotype deconstruction*.

3. The discourse identified as the *bonding (seduction-in-interaction) discourse* shares much in common with *relationship-oriented seduction strategies* (Bianchi et al., 2005). This discourse is characteristically associated with open, natural behaviour where nothing is hidden and the actors truthfully reveal their intentions.

The other three discourses—*influencing fate, non-existence of seduction* and the *pressure discourse*—do not appear to overlap with the discourses identified within the majority population and may be specific minority discourses, Roma discourses.

Moreover, the discourses on seduction can be meaningfully linked to the subjective meanings of sex in heterosexual relationships categorized in Supeková and Bianchi (2000) (see Sect. 3.3.1). The construction of seduction as a gradual process of getting to know the other person, motivated by a desire for intimacy corresponds to the *meaning of sex as an activity associated with intimacy and partnership*. A further two meanings of sex— *sex associated with personal pleasure* and *sex as a means of improving self-image*—correspond to dimensions of the *consumerist discourse*. In this type of discourse, seductive activities aimed at the "consumption" of as many interactions as possible are motivated out of a desire to raise self-esteem and gain experiences. However, in this study we did not find sex constructed as an activity that is *more about pleasing one's partner than a source of personal enjoyment*.

Given the many similarities, it seems likely that many of the discursive resources that young people draw on in their ideas about sexuality, and which form the psychological dimension of sexual behaviour, are common to both the majority and minority populations. This "convergence" of sexual subjectivity is in line with the transformational trends evident among Roma families as described in Čonková (2004) (see also Krajčovičová, 2009) and/or the growing proportion of type-one families (the most socially integrated family type) and the declining proportion of type-three families (families living in traditional gender communities, parents working occasionally, children not being sent to school, frequent change of housing), which differ enormously in the extent to which they exhibit the patriarchal asymmetries that facilitate sexual-health risks.

5.3　Epistemological Triangulation in the Study of Sexual Subjectivity

As one of the pioneers of qualitative research in psychology in the Czech and Slovak scientific community during the 1990s I was invited to participate in a summarizing-visioning debate among senior researchers (ex-pioneering and current leading) on qualitative research in psychology under the title *Establishing* [new research methodology] *Does Not Mean You Are Free of Responsibility: Promises and Present State of Qualitative Research in Czechia and Slovakia* (Masaryk et al., 2017). It should be pointed out that in this era (1989–) the Marxist theory of knowledge (Lenin's reflexive theory) and the materialist paradigm accepting positivist psychology (e.g. social-learning theory) that were the only allowed theoretical frameworks for psychology during the previous 40 years of communist regime were being challenged by alternative psychological paradigms that built on the linguistic turn—social constructivism and other critical approaches. These brought a number of new paradigms and methodological approaches into the, by then, rigid intellectual arena, e.g. social representations theory, theory of identity, various approaches to the analysis of discourse and Q-methodology. Besides the introduction of qualitative epistemology and methodology into psychology in the Central European area, there was also the question of continuity with mainstream psychology (addressed, e.g. in Gondec & Bianchi, 2012). The crucial share of innovation was to be found in the integrative methodological approaches—originally in Q-methodology combined with the discursive epistemology (see above Sect. 5.2), but also in studies introducing an even broader epistemological triangulation which I, among many others, was generously invited to join (Schmitt et al., 2003a, b, 2004a, b).

I drew attention to this exciting and daring application of epistemological triangulation back in 2007 (Bianchi, 2008). Here I would like to introduce the scope of the diverse epistemological platforms that were triangulated via correlational (variation) analytics. This triangulation added some illustrations of the knowledge assets towards sexual subjectivity.

The diverse epistemological platforms integrated in the studies were:

1. Evolutionary theory/psychology (Buss and Schmitt's (1993) sexual strategies theory, theory of parental investments (Trivers, 1972), and strategic pluralism theory (Gangestad & Simpson, 2000))
2. Developmental psychology (Bowlby's ethological theory of attachment (Feeney, 1994), and, based on it, Bartholomew and Horwitz's (1991) theory of romantic attachment styles: *secure, preoccupied, dismissing and fearful*
3. Positivist reified conceptualization of psychic phenomena (measurement of personality traits according to the Big Five theory (Benet-Martínez & John, 1998))
4. Behavioural and self-assessment measures/scales focusing on erotics and sexuality
5. Socio-cultural moderation (socio-cultural structural theory (Eagly & Wood, 1999)), exemplified by, e.g. Hofstede's cultural masculinity index, gender equity index, gender empowerment measure (percentage of women in governance)
6. Environmental stress factors (Taylor et al., 2000) (national fertility rate, human development index (HDI) and per capita gross domestic product (GDP))

Despite these studies (Schmitt et al., 2003a, b, 2004a, b) attracting the broad interest of the scientific community based on the appealing topic (sexual conduct), with at least 100 citations for each, there was insufficient acknowledgement of their epistemological contribution. These studies ask questions about the universality of patterns of adult romantic attachment, systematic sex/gender differences in the prevalence of the dismissing attachment style, the universality and patterns of mate poaching and differences in the desire for sexual variety. The findings clearly confirm the well-founded design of the studies based on the confrontation of various epistemological sources and assessment of the predictive potential of complex sexual behaviour. The studies obtained several findings documenting the interaction between evolutionary, essentialist psychological, and cultural phenomena; these phenomena were identifiable mainly owing to the use of epistemological triangulation in the studies. The main findings were:

1. Romantic Attachment Styles

   – Despite the "almost universally" valid model of positive/negative self-image and image of the other(s) among cultures and **all four romantic-attachment styles (secure, preoccupied, dismissing and fearful) can be observed across all cultures,** and
   – the fact that **secure attachment style** (conditioned by having a positive image of oneself and the other(s)) is the most frequent of four styles in 49 cultures (i.e. 79% of cultures included in the studies),
   – **the East-Asian samples had a significantly higher score in preoccupied romantic attachment style** (low self-image, exaggerated image of the other) than all the other cultures,
   – **and samples from countries with low economic, educational and healthcare rankings (according to HDI)** showed more frequent occurrence of preoccupied, dismissing and fearful romantic attachment style than did countries with a high HDI; however, prevalence of a secure romantic attachment style did not correlate with HDI level; life-stress conditions (e.g. high fertility rate) and/ or low HDI are predictors of increased "unsecure" romantic attachment styles (Schmitt et al., 2004a).

2. Mate Poaching
   Despite mate poaching attracting and stealing a sexual partner from another relationship (be it for short-term or long-term mating) being culturally universal, and poachers and the objects of poaching having almost identical personality profiles (characterized by high extraversion, openness and erotophilia, and low agreeableness), some aspects of mate poaching are related to aspects of culture:

   - **prevalence of mate poaching,** the individual incidence of mate poaching, as well as succumbing to attempts at mate poaching, is significantly higher in males than females in all cultural regions of the world (the only exception being Oceania for long-term mating), which confirms the **evolutionary sexual strategies theory**;
   - also, the success rate of male short-term mate poaching is significantly higher than in female mate poaching;
   - the prevalence of mate poaching in women, as well as succumbing to mate poaching (both for short-term and long-term mating), correlates negatively with per capita GDP (giving support for **the evolutionary strategic pluralism theory:** the lower the economic status of the environment, the higher the potential for women to activate the second selective strategy—to switch from the father of children to searching for an economically stronger provider of care for the children);
   - the **social structural theory** was partially confirmed by findings of a positive correlation between the Gender Equity Index and the prevalence of short-term mate poaching in women (Schmitt et al., 2004b).

3. Male Dominance in Dismissing Attachment Style
   There were two sets of hypotheses concerning the distribution of dismissing romantic attachment. The first hypothesis concerned the global distribution of the higher prevalence of men dismissing romantic attachment compared to women—driven by both evolutionary (E) and social role (S) arguments:

   - The first hypothesis postulated that **gender differences in dismissing romantic attachment exist across most cultures** based on the presumption that (E) men are generally more oriented towards short-term mating via indiscriminate sex than women are, and dismissing romantic attachment in adults is indicative of short-term mating tendencies; moreover (S) gender differences in dismissing romantic attachment are an expected consequence of women having universally adopted the social role of nurturer.

Higher scores for dismissing romantic attachment style in men than women were found in almost all the world's cultural regions—except for Africa, Oceania and Eastern Asia, with no significant gender differences. Thus the combined evolutionary/ social role hypotheses of a specific male sexual strategy (short-term mating) were confirmed to a large extent.

- The second hypothesis concerned the **decrease in gender differences in dismissing romantic attachment for both evolutionary (E) and social role (S) reasons**:

   Gender differences in dismissing romantic attachment will be smaller (E) in cultures with high-stress environments, based on the notion that reproductively stressful environments trigger women's tendency towards short-term mating, including the adaptive desire for briefly mating with men who possess "good genes"; moreover (S) gender differences in dismissing romantic attachment will be smaller in cultures with modern or progressive sex-role ideologies and where women have access to political and economic power.

   This complex hypothesis was partly confirmed by the finding that the extent of sex differences in dismissing attachment style correlated negatively with the fertility rate indicator. The socio-cultural hypothesis that higher sex differences in dismissing style are related to a higher masculinity score for the given culture was not confirmed and women's greater access to economic and political power was associated with greater differences between men and women—the opposite of the expected direction (Schmitt et al., 2003b).

4. Desire for Sexual Variety

   The study brought clear evidence of a constant, universal difference between male and female sexual mating strategies with a **significantly higher desire for sexual variety (number of desired sexual partners for short-term and long-term mating) in males in all cultures**. This endorses the evolutionary explanation of the difference (Schmitt et al., 2003a).

This set of studies is a useful illustration for several reasons. It shows that:

- It is possible to design a research study that confronts fundamentally different theoretical assumptions and to observe how these interact in the data obtained.
- It is fruitful to conduct research triangulating methods as well as diverse epistemological and even ontological bases—in order to obtain information documenting human nature, and our subjectivity, in a genuinely psychological way, and aspiring to the expectations of second-order psychology (Brown & Stenner, 2009).
- And last, not least, it emphasizes the primary importance of thinking in terms of theory. Theory-driven research strategies may result in a design which acknowledges that competing explanatory arenas may produce synergic hypothetical expectations!

5.4   "Advanced Thinking" for Social Sciences and Humanities

We are getting very close to the end of this book. The purpose of this last chapter is to present some methodological directions that may prove useful when searching for new tools to pursue our interests in psychological subjectivity and second-order psychological thinking.

What do I mean by "advanced thinking" in the title of this chapter? Psychologist have for decades, actually almost from the very beginning of "institutionalized psychology," been divided into epistemological territories separated off from one another by relatively high walls. Wundt's mentalism, Freud's psychoanalysis, Skinner's behaviourism, the mainstream (materialist) essentialism of psychological traits and capacities/abilities, the social constructivism that builds on the linguistic turn, critical theory, the discursive paradigm, to mention just the main streams, are rarely unleashed from behind their walls. Therefore, looking outside the box (or better put, "looking outside the walls") may be a good way for researchers and theorists to overcome the limitations of each and every psychological epistemology. This is especially worthwhile because epistemological "platforms" have developed outside of psychology that could be introduced into our own specific scientific discipline and that could offer progressive thinking on the enduring problems and dilemmas within the discipline. And, of course, it could help us in our exploration of the complexity of human subjectivity and search for predictors of improvements to our condition.

I have had the opportunity of using some of these innovative methodological directions—in research or in practice, while others were encountered as I snuck around looking for new ways of improving psychological knowingness. These are mainly:

A. The positive deviance paradigm
B. Psychotherapy as related to subjectivity
C. From assemblages to predictions—exploiting design thinking, systems thinking and modelling

It is important to mention that most of these innovations do not originate in psychology itself (positive deviance approach, design thinking, systems thinking, liminality hotspot, agency) but come from different—more or less remote—disciplines: nutrition science, architecture, environmental science, cultural anthropology, philosophy. Each of them, however, constitutes a significant challenge for psychological thinking.

5.4.1   Positive Deviance—Highlighting the Power of Non-normative Subjectivity—Contrasting Community Norms

The positive deviance approach was described, applied and observed by Jerry and Monique Sternin in the early 1990s when trying to improve the widespread malnutrition in children in Vietnam (Singhal, Greiner, and Dura, 2010). As they had limited financial resources and a short-term Vietnamese permit, they tried to find an alternative approach. The Sternins focused their attention on minority children who were not suffering from malnutrition despite their families being among the average poor farmers in the villages. Soon they noticed similar feeding patterns among the mothers of these children—compared to the traditional feeding culture in the communities. Most of these families with well-fed children lived outside of the villages as a consequence of being "expelled" due to the fact that the majority perceived them as deviant (Le Thi,[8] 2019). The "positively deviant" feeding pattern differed from the traditional/majority feeding pattern mainly in the distribution of food into several smaller portions during the day, prevention of food waste, addition of sweet-water

---

[8] In 2019 I had the opportunity to speak in person with Le Thi Nga who, as a linguistic and cultural translator, was crucial for the success of Sternins' involvement in the rural environment.

shrimp (rich in protein) to the rice dishes. This analytical phase was followed by a second stage implementing the positive deviance approach, which consisted of convincing and "teaching" the majority mothers the deviant minority feeding approach. Sternins achieved an incredible 50–80% improvement in nutrition in the communities they worked in—by using no additional resources and just transforming the community/cultural feeding norm into the direction of a "deviant" approach. This required subjective identification of members of the majority with norms of members of the "deviant" minority.

Later this approach, entailing a search for positive deviance behavioural patterns and solutions to community-related problems, was successfully studied and applied in contexts as diverse as the following (Kövérová, 2016, 2021; Singhal & Dura, 2009; Singhal, Buscell, and Lindberg, 2010):

- Hospital-acquired infections and other medical problems
- Stimulation of micro-loan economy
- Community inclusion of ex-war sex workers
- Prevention of secondary-school drop-outs due to unplanned pregnancy in teenage girls
- Educational success in marginalized, socially disadvantaged Roma youth

In general, these studies and projects on positive deviance all share the following common aspects:

- Form part of a complex social system
- Call for both social and behavioural change
- Entail solutions where the outcome may be uncertain and unpredictable

If we turn our mind back to psychological subjectivity this excursion into the positive deviance paradigm may prove inspirational. That could mean analysing and taking inspiration from those who do not correspond to the majority "norm," e.g. (a) failing to complete secondary education due to belonging to a marginalized and socially disadvantaged ethnic minority, (b) suffering from unwanted sexual attention, (c) living an environmentally unsustainable life, (d) lacking educational resources for personal growth or (e) the health risks of an unhealthy diet. In other words, learning from the "deviants" who, contrary to the majority norm, e.g. (a) manage to complete secondary education despite the unfavourable circumstances, (b) in terms of sexual subjectivity, cope well with sexual violence and abuse on the internet and in the social media, (c) learn from those with environmentally sound subjectivity who pursue a sustainable yet fun lifestyle, (d) learn from those who actively develop their reading skills and critical thinking capacity or (e) learn from those who avoid the obesity associated with junk food and junk lifestyles and have a health subjectivity.

5.4.2   Psychotherapy in Relation to Subjectivity

This section merely points out the importance of paying attention to psychotherapy when considering the importance of subjectivity. Neither the theory nor the practice of psychotherapy falls within my field of expertise. Therefore I would welcome any attempts by a qualified, determined scholar interested in delving into the many kinds of psychotherapeutic approaches that appear at times to either pretend embracing each other, resulting in various kinds of hybrid, eclectic or holistic approaches combining elements of several psychotherapeutic schools, or drown when directly confronted with "competing" approaches (cf. Patterson, 1980). The purpose of this endeavour would be to retrieve the psychological subject from each psychotherapeutic conception of the human being. At first glance, the expectations, trust and capacity of the subject varies substantially according to the psychotherapeutic approach—at the extreme low end we have Rational and Learning Theory approaches, and at the extreme high end we have Client-Centred and Existential approaches. The psychological subject should be at the centre of psychotherapeutic efforts for them to work effectively.

5.4.3   From Assemblages to Predictions—Exploiting Design Thinking, Systems Thinking and Modelling

In this section on advanced thinking I will not proceed quite as far beyond conventional epistemologies as Deleuze and Guattari (1987) do in their psychoanalytically inspired rhizomatic epistemology reach. Deleuze and Guatarri's philosophy emphasizes the importance of multiplicity and heterogeneity in understanding reality and society. Their psycho-analytical approach suggests that the innate motivation of people and society, their desires, is that of infinite possibility and multiplicity, of constantly becoming something rather than achieving a fixed state (*knowingness*?). Assemblages are not stable, but fluid and constantly becoming, temporally bounded spaces of associated multiplicity, unified to satisfy desire. Our knowledge emerges in assemblages, i.e. representations of multiplicity and heterogeneity, a non-hierarchical, fluid network of disparate objects and associations.[9] Irwin and Michael (2003, p. 108) drew on Deleuze and Guattari's concept of assemblage, suggesting that *ethno-epistemic assemblages* or rather conflicting ethno-epistemic assemblages be used for diverse (contradictory) interpretations of the complexity of the world. An ethno-epistemic assemblage combines the individual's context (ethnos) and the forms of knowledge relevant to their contexts (episteme) in assemblages, highlighting the interwoven, dynamic and fluid nature of (a specific) episteme against and in conjunction with other ethno-epistemic assemblages and social narratives (Lee, 2015).

As a means of linguistically/textually representing complex societal phenomena, ethno-epistemic assemblages may resemble the theory of social representations (Moscovici, 1961, 2001), but above all the discursive approach and the textuality and tectonics of discourses (Curt, 1994). The discursive resources approach (Willig, 1993, p. 384) highlights the agency, position and construction of the subjectivity of a subject involved in and exploiting any discourse. The ethno-epistemic assemblage approach is distinct from the platform of discourses, narratives and/or scripts; it is more dynamic as it highlights individual expectations/desires for the future and thus has fruitful analytical implications for the study of publics. However, the rhizomatic epistemology of ethno-epistemic assemblages does not entail rational reduction of the vast textual complexity of discourses into predictive models. Therefore, in search of a more productive approach, in a recent paper (Šviráková & Bianchi, 2018), we presented an integrative methodology for social sciences and humanities based on three

---

[9] An assemblage, in its multiplicity, necessarily acts on semiotic flows, material flows and social flows simultaneously (independently of any recapitulation that may be made of it in a scientific or theoretical corpus). There is no longer a tripartite division between a field of reality (the world) and a field of representation (the book) and a field of subjectivity (the author). Rather, an assemblage establishes connections between certain multiplicities drawn from each of these orders, so that a book has no sequel nor the world as its object nor one or several authors as its subject. In short, we think that one cannot write sufficiently in the name of an outside. The outside has no image, no signification, no subjectivity. The book as assemblage with the outside, against the book as image of the world. A rhizome book, not a dichotomous, pivotal or fascicular book (Deleuze & Guattari, 1987, p. 22–23).

methodological-strategic models and theories that are well-established in natural and technical sciences, and the arts. This approach combines design thinking (Lawson, 1980), systems approach (systems theory, von Bertalanffy, 1968),systems thinking (Meadows et al., 1972; Meadows, 2008) and system dynamics modelling (Forrester, 1971) as methodological platforms for analysing large amounts of qualitative data and transforming it into a quantitative mode with predictive output. Moreover, the aim is to reveal causality in research on societal and behavioural issues. I propose this approach should be given the working title *design-systems-dynamic-modelling* and I will now outline its rationale in "simple form."

Since the publication of Bryan Lawson's *How Designers Think* (1980) there has been a significant shift in the theory of knowledge: in design thinking the ambition is to move the focus away from "problem (driven) thinking" and onto "solution/need (driven) thinking." Production models and prototypes are part of the design process (Ambrose et al., 2011; Knapp et al., 2016). Product designers use models and prototypes to verify the extent to which the design meets customer demands. The logical chain in the design-thinking approach starts from a needs assessment and based on that solution(s) are proposed. These model solutions are then materialized into prototypes. The prototypes are tested and then entered into final production or service delivery.

Design thinking has gradually moved away from the material environment and towards economics and social issues. Key educational institutions have introduced design thinking as a universal methodology for numerous scientific disciplines including social sciences (e.g. service design, or the communication design courses offered at Politecnico di Milano). Tackling societal problems via the proposal of possible solutions instead of analysing problems as entities[10] is becoming increasingly popular.

To illustrate possible applications of design thinking in behavioural science, we can take the situation of children and young teenagers exploring their sexual subjectivity. Lacking open communication about sexuality and intimacy with adults and teachers, they frequently fall victim to sexual misinformation and abuse on the internet, which leads to shame, fear and trauma. The traditional, problem-oriented approach is to protect children

---

[10] Actually, despite being rooted in peak modernity, this approach is typical of late modernity/post-modernity, reflecting the general deviation away from rationality towards forwardness, sensuality and emotionality in thinking (cf. Maffesoli, 2006).

on the internet via monitoring, surveillance, censorship, threats and punishments. In contrast the design-thinking approach starts with the identification of needs, in this case the inherent curiosity and urges that are a natural part of bodily, social and personal maturation (subjectivization). In this approach, different solution designs would be developed for this situation: open communication/dialogue through encouraging parents and training teachers on sexuality and intimacy. The saturation of primary needs reinforces the young person's subject and strengthens resistance to the manipulative power of the internet.

In analytical thinking, models and theories are the highest level of abstraction. According to Sterman (1991), we create and use mental models daily without realizing it. Our decision-making and actions are not based on the real world but on intuitive mental images of the external world, weighing relationships between the different elements, ideas and the possible consequences of our actions (causality). However, it is hard to interpret mental models—the tentative designs/solutions that might satisfy our needs—comprehensively and unequivocally. Computer modelling enables us to systematically assess behaviours occurring within a particular process observed in the social environment. It can be used to evaluate a variety of decision-strategies and predict behaviour in any social and economic system. Computer models process the logical consequences of all the conditions entered into the model. Computer models are comprehensible and can process many factors simultaneously and display them on a timeline. Such models are quantitative abstractions of qualitative relations.

The central concept that sets our approach apart from traditional thinking is design thinking. The role of the design is objectified in the model and there are two levels of model available. On the first level there are individual "mental" models representing solutions to people's needs. By collecting data from numerous individual models (using any data available—interviews and quantitative assessments) concerning possible solutions and submitting the data to structured analysis, we obtain the inputs to compute a system-dynamics model that can predict the possible outcomes of the system. The analytical process, from gathering the individuals' models to the final outcome, consists of open, axial and selective coding (in the framework of a rigorous grounded theory approach), followed by the creation of a causal loop diagram highlighting the causal relations of the identified categories in the system. Subsequently the central categories (variables) are entered into a system-dynamic computation resulting in a system-dynamic model that predicts the possible outcomes of the system dynamics depending on the variation in the specific categories and their causal interactions. The computed system dynamics model is an elaborate version of the participants' original mental models. It builds on a systematic analysis of the original mental models.

As an example I will describe two of the steps in the pilot study we conducted recently (Šviráková & Bianchi, 2018). The aim was to identify the main problems with a work-flow in a university design studio and propose solutions that would lead to a high quality studio product. The primary empirical data on the work-flow were collected via questionnaires and interviews with all participants in the studio. The open coding (which produced seven categories of concepts/variables (A–G, shown in Fig. 5.2) and axial coding were performed. The aim of the axial coding is to identify possible causal relations between categories, identified through the coincidence of items. We identified 11 separate causal relations between the categories. These causalities indicate relations between singular categories only. The next step—selective coding—was performed in order to find interconnections between the categories.

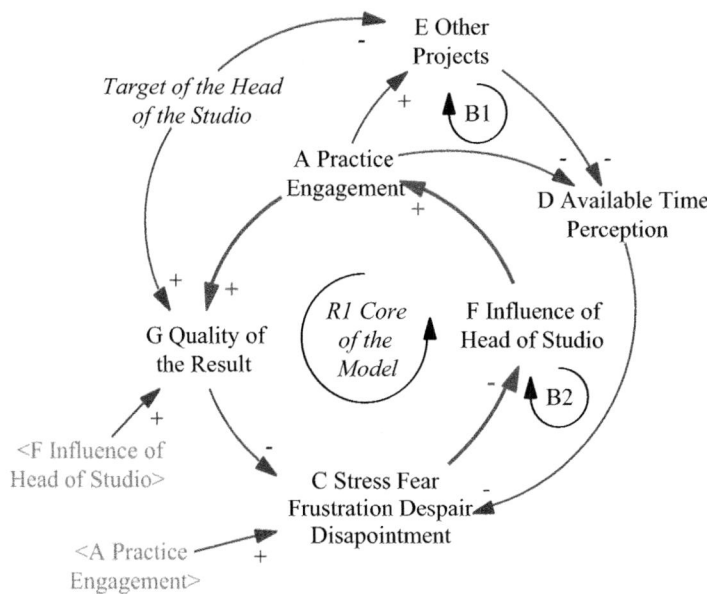

Fig. 5.2 Causal loop diagram (Šviráková & Bianchi, 2018)

These three coding steps are a comprehensive way of creating a grounded theory in order to identify the causal relations among categories. This was followed by the system-thinking procedure. In practice this means designing the causal loop diagram of positive and negative feedbacks among the categories (Fig. 5.2). The identified loops determine the system and the dynamic hypotheses. In our case the hypotheses were as follows: the studio head has a strong influence over the studio (*F Influence of Studio Head*) and fosters stronger collaboration between the students and external companies (*Practical Experience*). This ensures a higher quality result (*G Quality of Outcome*), and in turn reduces the students' stress (*C Stress Fear Frustration Despair Disappointment*). Under less stress, the students consulted the studio head more, reinforcing the head's influence on the outcome of the studio work. The head involves other companies so the students can work with other stakeholders/companies giving their work a more practical focus and improving the quality of their work.

Finally, the dynamic hypotheses resulting from the previous analytical processes had to be tested in order to answer the question: *How do the categories/variables mutually interact over time—what is the expected final "constellation" of the causal interactions?* This was done when computing the system dynamics (SD) model. The SD model is based on the causal loop diagram (CLD) and the stock and flow dynamics (Forrester, 1971). The model, computed with iterations for 30 weeks (equivalent to two semesters of the design course) (Fig. 5.3), confirmed that the studio head exerted a strong influence over the studio (*F Influence of Studio Head*), ensuring a more intensive relationship between the students and practical experience (*Practical Experience*). Both categories show dynamic growth. Growth in practical experience is accompanied by a higher quality outcome (*G Quality of the Outcome*), and the improvements in product quality reduce the students' stress (*C Stress Fear Frustration Despair Disappointment*). In turn the reduced stress leads to the students consulting the studio head more, which increases the head's influence on the outcome of the studio's work.

The aim of the pilot study was to visualize an integral (mixed) research procedure informed by design thinking—a solution-oriented approach applicable in the social sciences and humanities. The purpose of the procedure is to analyse situations requiring taking into account the information contained in a large amount of qualitative as well as quantitative data in

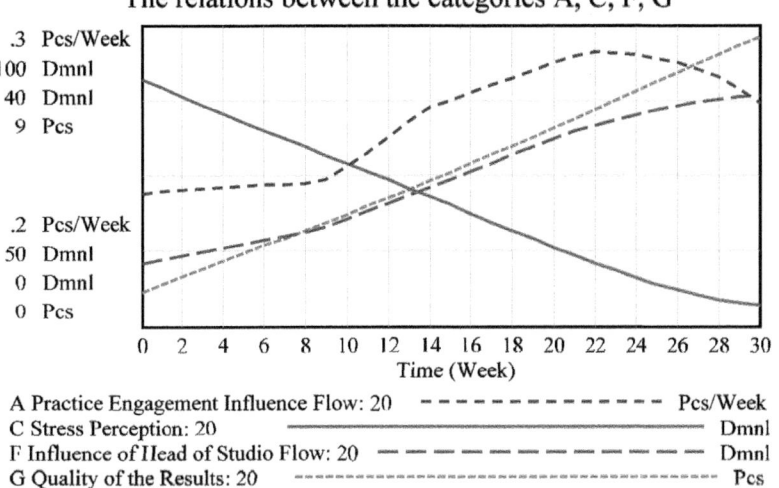

The relations between the categories A, C, F, G

A Practice Engagement Influence Flow: 20   – – – – – – – – – – – – –   Pcs/Week
C Stress Perception: 20   ————————————————   Dmnl
F Influence of Head of Studio Flow: 20   – – – – – – – – – – – – –   Dmnl
G Quality of the Results: 20   -------------------------------------   Pcs

Fig. 5.3 Studio head's target of 20 pieces. Own source, 2018. (The variable studio head's target is set at 20 products/pieces. This means the studio head is supposed to deliver 20 innovative products over 30 weeks). (Šviráková & Bianchi 2018)

order to formulate a bottom-up-driven explanation and solution. More specifically, it is about creating a system dynamics model that enables us to verify the comprehensive mental modelling of solutions to a complex problem. In general, it builds on and contributes to people's subjectivity, which is both an essential building element in the procedure, as well as the main target to be addressed in its evolution.

More specifically, it is about creating a system dynamics model that enables us to verify the comprehensive mental modelling of solutions to a complex problem. Thus, it is possible to obtain a comprehensive causal understanding of complex social systems (which also may have their own subjectivity) that takes into account the dynamics of the subjectivities of multiple actors in their diverse roles and positions. And this in turn brings us closer to the goals of second-order psychology.

SUMMARY

This was a sort of "tour de force" with a strong biographic footprint. I would like to conclude by saying that introducing all the innovative approaches to the scientific community in Slovakia was extremely exciting on the one hand but—very often—extremely tiring on the other. My colleagues and I regularly had to fight against traditional institutions that operated as bastions seeking to protect mainstream psychology from "dangerous" innovations.

CHAPTER 6

Instead of a Conclusion—A New Starting Point? Liminality and Agency—The Gateway to Authentic Subjectivity? Liminality Hotspots as a Special Case for "Extended/Expanded/Augmented" Subjectivity? And a Pessimistic Teaser at the End—Is Our Own (Conscious) Subjectivity the Key Obstacle to Understanding Others' Subjectivity?

Abstract The final chapter of this tiny book is an attempt to return to the very beginning, where I tried to justify the urgent need to find more complex concepts—assuming that psychology aspires to be a good authority on understanding people in all their complexity—in particular the need to grasp human subjectivity in its diversity, plurality, self-generativity and livedness (it has to be lived). To capture the process (dynamics) of becoming a psychological subject I suggest we draw on the emerging conceptualization of liminality and liminality hotspots and psychological agency. But thinking further, it is as if an epistemological ghost has appeared to tease us, prompting us to wonder if our own conscious subjectivity is the key obstacle to (properly) understanding other people's subjectivity and that human subjectivity will remain unknowable, non-negotiable and incompatible.

I understand these endeavours as a step in the right direction towards second-order psychology (Brown & Stenner, 2009). In fact, this shift may have some of the attributes of a paradigm shift in psychology as discussed by Kuhn (1970/1996)—leaving aside the fact that Kuhn doubted the possibility of a paradigm emerging in the social sciences. According to Kuhn, such a shift would cast doubt on any facts and methods obtained under the previous paradigm. To continue in this direction would require a complex and deep analysis of all mainstream psychology laws and theories, which is not my intention in this book. Nonetheless the question remains open.

Following our excursion around the variations of figurations of human subjectivity (encompassing our values, cultural and political subjectivity, sexuality, intimacy, gender and norms in general) and some of the alternative epistemological/methodological approaches for capturing subjectivity, I attempt here to capture the process (dynamics) of becoming a psychological subject by drawing on the emerging conceptualization of *liminality* and *liminality hotspots.*

In the last decade of critical psychology our attention has been directed towards the concept of liminality, among other things. Stenner (2017) has outlined the concept of liminality in the context of the emerging awareness of "the psychosocial"—the psychosocial is *"the relation between societal processes and subjective experience"* (ibid, p. 1). The subject with his/her/its/their experiences thus takes centre place in our attention along with the societal environment and mutual interactions. Thus when we think about the human subject, all aspects of the societal environment are a valid subject for consideration. But why does Stenner turn our attention to liminality?

Originally the focus was very much on French anthropologist and ethnologist Arnold Kurr van Gennep's critical reading and his study on the rites of passage, in which he identified the crucial importance of liminal situations (van Gennep, 1909/1960) in the transition from one recognized "position" or "structure" to another (e.g. from child to adult). Then Stenner contributed some psychoanalytical inputs: (1) D.W. Winnicot's (1953) view on how our selfhood emerges in liminal transitions from childhood, and (2) Deleuze and Guattari's (1987) understanding of the adult's (men's) becomings of new subjectivity.

With regard to Winnicot's view of the self/subject, Stenner (2017, p. 17–18) states that

> "we cannot start with 'the self' but must explain its emergence. The 'self' is not first of all the subject of experience but the effect or result of experience … this miracle of the emergence of a self is something each of us had to go through and something that is gone through every day by millions of infants. It is also not a once-and-for-all event, but a process, and it is a process that some of us may revisit (in a new way of course) even as adults. Winnicott shows us, or at least gives us profound insights into, how the self emerges from a liminal zone of indistinction."

Thus, Winnicot explains how our subjectivity expands towards final selfhood by extending our social world (collective, community), developing our creativity and play (art and intellectual performance) and constructing our religiosity/spirituality or science.

Episodes of liminal experiences, significant transition, passage or disruption, that occur during the process of acquiring a new subjectivity, can be found in the approach of Deleuze and Guattari (1987) who call them *becomings*. However, Deleuze and Guattari (1987) limit becoming to the process of acquiring any minority subjectivity: "*Why are there so many becomings of man, but no becoming-man? First because man is majoritarian par excellence, whereas becomings are minoritarian; all becoming is a becoming-minoritarian. (p. 291) … There is no becoming-man because man is the molar entity par excellence, whereas becomings are molecular … the standard upon which the majority is based: (is) white, male, adult, rational, etc., in short, the average European, the subject of enunciation (p292)."*

Hence experiences that take place in a zone liminal to our current self/subjectivity are a necessary part of becoming an adult, and where the person is already an adult, becoming a new subject.

We experience liminality when … our lives are, for some reason, disrupted, interrupted, transformed or suspended. (Stenner, 2017, p. 14)

Greco and Stenner (2017) call such transitions "pattern shifts," one could perhaps say life-pattern transitions, and such transitions may challenge our subjectivity.

According to Stenner (2017, p. 15), liminal experiences are of two types: (1) *spontaneous* liminal experiences (events that befall us or that *happen to us*) and (2) *devised* or *fabulated* liminal experiences (performative events that we proactively "do to ourselves" in the sense that we artfully contrive the liminal experience). This duality raises an additional question regarding the need for agency—a concept that has recently been hijacked from philosophy. In particular, the second type of liminal experience—*devised or fabulated* experiences—requires the agency of the subject, e.g. when taking part in a challenging test, a risky sport activity or an unsafe intimate adventure. In the end Stenner proposes a dialectic and dynamic understanding of the role of liminality in human life that results in "*a view of human life as liminal in the sense of being* **constituted by boundaries which are then transcended**" [bold added] (ibid, p. 31). So what are the most progressive exploitations of agency in psychology?

Agency—The Self as Agent—Psychology and the Question of Agency—Psychological Agency: Theory, Practice and Culture
These are the titles of four inspiring texts introducing and elaborating on the concept of agency in contemporary psychology. *The Self and the Agent* is a book by the Scottish philosopher John Macmurray from 1957, "Agency," by the American philosopher Donald Davidson,[1] is the initial chapter in *Agent, Action, and Reason* (1971), edited by Binkley, Bronaugh and Marras. The third is the pioneering manifesto *Psychology and the Question of Agency* (2003) by the psychologists Martin, Sugarman and Thompson, drawing on the concept of agency into psychological thought, and the fourth is a comprehensive psychological exploration of the concept of agency—*Psychological Agency: Theory, Practice, and Culture* (2008a)—edited by Roger Frie.
Frie, in his introductory chapter to the volume offers a conceptual view of agency in psychology (Frie, 2008b). Current interpretations of agency see it as an active form of participation, the manifestation of power and/or a form of resistance/defence/achievement. Frie, however, pleads for a complex conception of agency. Incorporating agency into psychological theory and practice could play a crucial role in efforts

(continued)

---

[1] Davidson's thinking was introduced to Slovak readers by Emil Višňovský, 2009: *Človek ako homo agens. Bratislava, Iris.*

(continued)

to overcome the ontological and epistemological abyss between modernity (positivisms) and postmodernity (critical theory) in psychology:

> agency as a central feature of the relational, embodied person, embedded within dynamically evolving social and interactive circumstances. ...agency and self-experience **transcends the distinction between modernist certainty and postmodernist fragmentation**... agency is not reducible to biophysical properties, or to depersonalized social and cultural forces. And in the wake of widely held conceptions that equate agency with Western and gender-biased notions of individuality and autonomy... agency is not an isolated act of detached self-reflection and choice. The objective, rather, is to reconfigure agency as an emergent and developmental process that is fundamentally **intersubjective and contextualized**. (*bold* added) (Frie, 2008b, p. 2)

The crucial link between agency and subjectivity (understanding oneself as an agent; agency as the essence of the self-developing subjectivity) is expressed by Frie thus:

> *Change is based on an openness to new possibilities of being. When we come to understand ourselves as agents in our world, it becomes possible for us to imagine making different choices, and to relate to others and act in different ways.* (Frie, 2008b, p.13)

Frie shows that among numerous scholars from diverse backgrounds there is a characteristic agreement on positive value attribution to agency—mainly due to the aspects of possibility for choice and independence of the subject aiming at a state where people are authors of their quality.

Sugarman stresses special ontological agency when speaking about "*agentic being and becoming*" (Sugarman, 2008, p.81) and focuses on relational agency in particular, expanding the notion of individual subjectivity to include relational subjectivity.

> *agentic being and becoming are dependent on mutual relations with others.* (Sugarman, 2008, p. 81)

So, if liminality represents a zone of possibilities determined by the limits (of their present subjectivity) which people may approach, as well as by the possibility of crossing over, thanks to agency, into the new zone (and new subjectivity), with all the accompanying emotional excitement— *"liminal occasions tend to be highly affective in nature because they are formative moments of great significance: leaps into the unknown"* (Stenner, 2017, p.15). But what happens if the border is not crossed? Stenner and Clinch (2013) developed the concept of "liminal hotspots" to deal with that possibility.

6.1   Liminal Hotspots as a Special Case for "Extended/Expanded/Augmented" Subjectivity?

What is a liminal hotspot? A liminal hotspot is a mental/social/cultural/institutional state of being betwixt and between the old (current) and the new (future, potential) state of the subject. Greco and Stenner (2017) characterize liminal hotspots as paradox, paralysis, polarization and (potentially) a pattern shift. Here there is no smooth transition accompanying the rite of passage from one recognized "position" or "structure" to another— e.g. from childhood to adulthood. Instead people become "stuck" in transition, caught in a long-term (or even permanent) state of "in-betweenness" or transition. Examples can be found in numerous fields: the precarious labour conditions facing the unemployed—to be contrasted with stable employment, migrants relinquishing their original national identity and seeking a new identity in a host country, the treatment of a chronic illness—preventing a state of illness insufficience and still informing the subject of not being healthy. Another potential liminal hotspot is sexual interaction at a time when the sexual, social, moral and other norms that previously demarcated good from bad, safe from unsafe or wanted from unwanted are being deconstructed. As Greco and Stenner (2017) remind us, a liminal hotspot can have existential aspects. In extreme cases the subject may find themselves permanently stuck in the liminal hotspot.

These are my final thoughts on subjectivity in this small book. It would please me greatly if I have inspired readers to critically reflect on the glorified mound of knowledge, theories, principles and instruments created by mainstream (first order) psychology over almost 150 years since it was established in 1879. Let us hope that by reflecting on these the societal demand for psychological instruments will be replaced with a demand for knowledge about human subjectivity. No doubt there is currently a high and still rising societal demand on processes of subjectification:

individuals are being exhorted constantly to reflexively monitor themselves. We are invited to identify, measure and compare our desires, aspirations and behaviours against well-publicized but ever-changing norms that relate to every aspect of human life: our frequency and variety of types of sexual intercourse; the amount of time we spend with our children; the number of times we visit our doctor; the duration and nature of our experience of bereavement; the quantity of units of alcohol we consume in a week, etc. No area of life is immune. As Foucault pointed out, power in contemporary society operates increasingly through processes of subjectification in which self-regulation is paramount and the self is experienced as an ongoing biographical project to be worked on and disciplined. (Gill, 2003b, p. 36)

Nonetheless there is an opportunity here, albeit limited, for the devil's advocate to contest efforts to produce comprehensive thinking about human subjectivities. By this I mean the epistemological teaser prompting our minds to the (im)possibilities of properly understanding others' subjectivities because we have our own consciously perceived construction of subjectivities; and that construction hinders our ability to understand "what it is like" to be another person. Here I follow up on Thomas Nagel (2014) and his scepticism that we can understand another person's consciousness. Nagel emphasizes the importance of the subjective character of our experience: "It is not captured by any of the familiar, recently devised reductive analyses of the mental, for all of them are logically compatible with its absence. It is not analysable in terms of any explanatory system of functional states, or intentional states, since these could be ascribed to robots or automata that behaved like people though they experienced nothing" (Nagel, 2014, p. 436). Moreover—and in particular—Nagel warns us that even if we can understand others (*what it is like to be ...*), we can only understand "what it would be like for *me* to behave as a bat behaves. But that is not the question. I want to know what it is like for a *bat* to be a bat" (ibid, p. 439). Here we can substitute the bat (chosen by Nagel on purpose to amplify the distinction between subjectivities) with "other people." All our efforts to understand other people's subjectivities end in us knowing how WE (biased by all our subjective experiences) understand their subjectivities. But how do they understand their subjectivities for them? Will we ever learn?

SUMMARY

In this book I have tried to create an illustrative image of what psychology could offer if the original positivist ambitions of psychological science of the nineteenth century were to be cast aside and the ontological and epistemological starting points were to follow the psychosocial paradigm. The diverse, multiple, self-generating and lived subjectivity, captured and explained by innovative methodologies and daring conceptualizations (e.g. liminality, psychological agency and liminality hotspots) illustrated by some examples from my research, are just a handful of possible ways of enriching and deepening psychology's justification in this late-modern chaotic world of humankind.

REFERENCES

Albee, G. W. (1970). The uncertain future of clinical psychology. *American Psychologist, 25*, 1071–1080.

Alvesson, M., & Sköldber, K. (2000). *Reflexive methodology: New vistas for qualitative research.* SAGE.

Ambrose, G., & Harris, P. (2011). *The fundamentals of creative design.* AVA Publishing.

Ansuini, C. G., Fiddler-Woite, J., & Woite, R. S. (1996). The source, accuracy, and impact of initial sexuality information on lifetime wellness. *Adolescence, 31*, 283–289.

Arribas-Ayllon, M., & Walkerdine, V. (2008). Foucauldian discourse analysis. In C. Willig & W. Stainton-Rogers (Eds.), *The Sage handbook of qualitative research in psychology* (pp. 91–108). Sage Publications.

Bajos, N., Ducot, B., Spencer, B., & Spira, A. (1998). Trajectoires socio-sexuelles et comportement face au risque de transmission sexuelle di Sida. In N. Bajos, A. Ferrand, A. Giami, & A. Spira (Eds.), *La sexualité aux temps du Sida* (pp. 305–336). Presses Universitaires de France.

Baker, W. J. (1992). Positivism versus people: What should psychology be about? In C. W. Tolman (Ed.), *Positivism in psychology historical and contemporary problems* (pp. 9–16). Springer.

Bartholomew, K., & Horowitz, L. M. (1991). Attachment styles among young adults: A test of a four-category model. *Journal of Personality and Social Psychology, 61*(2), 226–244. https://doi.org/10.1037/0022-3514.61.2.226

Bauman, Z. (2003). *Liquid love: On the frailty of human bonds.* Polity Press; Distributed in the USA by Blackwell Pub.

© The Author(s), under exclusive license to Springer Nature Switzerland AG 2022
G. Bianchi, *Figurations of Human Subjectivity*,
https://doi.org/10.1007/978-3-031-19189-3

Benet-Martínez, V., & John, O. P. (1998). Los Cinco Grandes across cultures and ethnic groups: Multitrait-multimethod analyses of the Big Five in Spanish and English. *Journal of Personality and Social Psychology, 75*(3), 729–750. https://doi.org/10.1037/0022-3514.75.3.729

Berger, P. L., & Luckmann, T. (1966). *The social construction of reality: A treatise in the sociology of knowledge.* Anchor Books.

Bernik, I., & Hlebec, V. (2005). How did it happen the first time? Sexual initiation of secondary school students in seven postsocialist countries. In A. Štulhofer & T. Sandfort (Eds.), *Sexuality and gender in postcommunist Eastern Europe and Russia* (pp. 297–316). Haworth Press.

Bianchi, G. (2001). Sexuálne zdravie ako kultúrny, sociálny a politický jav. In G. Bianchi (Ed.), *Identita, zdravie a nová paradigma* (pp. 169–184). VEDA.

Bianchi, G. (2003a). Public sexuality and the intimate public (postmodern reflections on sexuality). *Human Affairs, 13*(1), 59–75.

Bianchi, G. (Ed.). (2003b). *Upgrade pre sexuálnu výchovu.* VEDA & KVSBK SAV.

Bianchi, G. (2008). Sexualita – medzi biologickou a kultúrnou evolúciou: kritický pohľad cez prizmu štúdií D.T. Schmitta a spol. In D. Marková (Ed.), *Sexuality: zborník príspevkov z prvej medzinárodnej konferencie realizovanej* (pp. 12–21). Gaudeamus.

Bianchi, G. (2010a). Intimacy: From transformation to transmutation. *Human Affairs-Postdisciplinary Humanities & Social Sciences Quarterly, 20*(1), 1–8. https://doi.org/10.2478/v10023-010-0001-4

Bianchi, G. (2010b). Sex medzi mužmi: medzi realitou a diskurzmi. In K. Záborská & I. Čermák (Eds.), *Kvalitativní přístup a metody ve vědách o člověku IX.: individualita a jedinečnost v kvalitativním výzkumu : sborník vybraných příspěvků* (pp. 145–152) Psychologický ústav AV ČR.

Bianchi, G. (2010c). O čom je sex medzi mužmi. In D. Marková (Ed.), *Sexuality III.: zborník vedeckých príspevkov* (pp. 8–16). Univerzita Konštantína Filozofa.

Bianchi, G. (2019). Attitudes to progressive gene therapies in Slovakia in the light of the ethical dimensions of human enhancement. In P. Sýkora (Ed.), *Promises and perils of emerging technologies for human condition: Voices from four postcommunist Central and East European countries* (pp. 165–182). Peter Lang GmbH.

Bianchi, G. (2020). *Sexuality: From intimacy to politics: With focus on Slovakia in the globalized world.* Berlin, Peter Lang.

Bianchi, G., & Fuskova, J. (2015). Representations of sexuality in the Slovak media – the case of politics and violence. *Annual of Language & Politics and Politics of Identity, 9*(1), 43–70.

Bianchi, G., & Fuskova, J. (2018). Limits in sexual interaction: A liminality hotspot, rather than an explicit boundary? The subjectivity of the boundary between wanted and unwanted sex. *Human Affairs-Postdisciplinary Humanities & Social Sciences Quarterly, 28*(2), 187–195. https://doi.org/10.1515/humaff-2018-0015

Bianchi, G., & Lášticová, B. (2004). Gender and sex aspects of multiple identities: Young women and men from Bratislava and Prague heading toward the EU. *Sociologia, 36*(3), 293–313.

Bianchi, G., & Lášticová, B. (2005). Hodnotový kontext kolektívnych identít v meniacej sa Európe. *Slovenský národopis, 53*(3), 285–297.

Bianchi, G., & Luha, J. (2010). Non-participation of survey respondents: Sexual and bodily otherness on the margin of public interest. *Sociologia, 42*(5), 548–563.

Bianchi, G., & Reháková, L. (2013). Konštrukcia hranice ne-želaného sexu [Construction of the border in un-wanted sex]. In A. Neusar & L. Vavrysová (Eds.), *Proceedings of the international conference on qualitative methods in Research in Humanities and Social Sciences Olomouc, Czech Republic 21.- 22. ledna 2013* (pp. 47–52). Univerzita Palackého v Olomouci.

Bianchi, G., & Rosová, V. (1992). Environment as a value: Intraindividual, inter-individual, and intercultural differences. In H. Svobodvá (Ed.), *Culture – nature – landscape: 2nd international conference: Cultural aspects of landscape* (pp. 37–45). District library, Municipal office.

Bianchi, G., Popper, M., Lukšík, I., & Supeková, M. (1997). Cultural and social background of sexual satisfaction in relation to risky sexual behaviour. In R. Roth (Ed.), *Psychologists facing the challenge of a global culture with human rights and mental health* (pp. 119–125). Pabst Science Publishers.

Bianchi, G., Popper, M., Lukšík, I., Supeková, M., & Stenner, P. (1999a). An attempt at constructing of strategies concerning sexuality by young people. *Československá psychologie, 43*(3), 231–252.

Bianchi, G., Popper, M., Lukšík, I., & Supeková, M. (1999b). *Q-metodológia – alternatívny spôsob skúmania sexuálneho zdravia.* KVSK SAV.

Bianchi, G., Popper, M., Lukšík, I., & Supeková, M. (2000). Interakcia sexuál-nych a drogových rizík zdravia vojakov základnej vojenskej služby: výsledky výskumu a odporúčania pre Armádu SR. KVSBK SAV.

Bianchi, G., Popper, M., Supeková, & Lukšík, I. (2002). Hodnoty v pozadí sexu-ality: intímne občianstvo a sexuálne zdravie. In J. Gajdošová (Ed.), *Áno psycho-logickému poradenstvu! Radšej osobnosť rozvíjať ako liečiť: zborník z celoštátnej odbornej konferencie.* KPP a CVaPP.

Bianchi, G., Popper, M., Szeghyová, P., & Lukšík, I. (2005). Analýza zdrojov diskurzu: prečo a ako. In M. Miovský, I. Čermák, & V. Chrz (Eds.), *Kvalitativní přístup ve vědách o člověku IV* (pp. 227–239). Univerzita Palackého v Olomouci.

Bianchi, G., Lášticová, B., & Šramová, B. (2007). Meanings of macro social cat-egories in Slovak adolescents: Between region and Europe. *Československá psy-chologie, 51*(5), 464–475.

Biel, J., Good, B., & Kleinman, A. (Eds.). (2007a). *Subjectivity: Ethnographic investigations.* University of California Press.

Biel, J., Good, B., & Kleinman, A. (2007b). Introduction: Rethinking subjectivity. In J. Biel, B. Good, & A. Kleinman (Eds.), *Subjectivity: Ethnographic investigations* (pp. 1–23). University of California Press.

Bird, S. T., & Harvey, S. M. (2000). "No Glove, No Love": Cultural beliefs of African-American women regarding influencing strategies for condom use. *International Quarterly of Community Health Education, 20*(3), 237–251. https://doi.org/10.2190/Q7MF-CR06-X4BU-4B4U

Blackman, L., Cromby, J., Hook, D., Papadopoulos, D., & Walkerdine, V. (2008). Creating subjectivities. *Subjectivity, 22*(1), 1–27. https://doi.org/10.1057/sub.2008.8

Bolfíková, E. (2003). Sexuálne a reprodukčné zdravie rómskej populácie (empirická analýza sexuálneho a reprodukčného správania rómskej populácie v oblasti Rožňava, Plešivec). *Člověk a Spoločnosť, 6*(3).

Borowiak, A. (2001). O czym mówimy, kiedy dyskutujemy o dyskursie postmodernistycznym? In I. Kurcz & J. Bobryk (Eds.), *Psychologiczne studia nad językiem i dyskursem* (pp. 141–175). Wydawnictwo Instytutu Psychologii PAN i Wydawnictwo SWPS Academica.

Bosá, M. (2017). Etika starostlivosti a starostlivá spoločnosť ako výzva pre sociálnu prácu [Ethics of care and caring society as a challenge for social work]. In B. Balogová (Ed.), *Šance a limity seniorov v súčasnej modernej komunikácii* (pp. 166–175). Prešovská Univerzita.

Boswell, J. (1994). *Same-sex unions in premodern Europe.* Villard Books.

Bozon, M., & Kontula, O. (1998). Sexual initiation and gender in Europe: A cross-cultural analysis of trends in the twentieth century. In M. Hubert, N. Bajos, & T. Sandfort (Eds.), *Sexual behaviour and HIV/AIDS in Europe* (pp. 37–67). UCL Press.

Braidotti, R. (2009). Postsecular feminist ethics. In E. H. Oleksy (Ed.), *Intimate citizenships: Gender, sexualities, politics* (pp. 40–62). Routledge.

Bronski, M. (1998). *The pleasure principle: Sex, backlash, and the struggle for gay freedom.* St. Martin's Press.

Brown, S. D., & Stenner, P. (2009). *Psychology without foundations.* SAGE Publications Ltd.

Bunčák, J. (2001). Religiozita na Slovensku a v európskom rámci. *Sociológia = Slovak sociological review: časopis pre otázky sociológie, 33*(1), 47–69.

Buss, D. M. (2006). Strategies of human mating. *Psihologijske Teme/Psychological Topics, 15*(2), 239–260.

Buss, D. M., & Schmitt, D. P. (1993). Sexual strategies theory: An evolutionary perspective on human mating. *Psychological Review, 100*(2), 204–232. https://doi.org/10.1037/0033-295X.100.2.204

Caprara, G. V., Vecchione, M., Schwartz, S. H., Schoen, H., Bain, P. G., Silvester, J., Cieciuch, J., Pavlopoulos, V., Bianchi, G., Kirmanoglu, H., Baslevent, C., Mamali, C., Manzi, J., Katayama, M., Posnova, T., Tabernero, C., Torres, C.,

Verkasalo, M., Lonnqvist, J. E., Vondrakova, E., & Caprara, M. G. (2017). Basic values, ideological self-placement, and voting: A cross-cultural study. *Cross-Cultural Research, 51*(4), 388–411. https://doi.org/10.1177/106939 7117712194

Caprara, G. V., Vecchione, M., Schwartz, S. H., Schoen, H., Bain, P. G., Silvester, J., Cieciuch, J., Pavlopoulos, V., Bianchi, G., Kirmanoglu, H., Baslevent, C., Mamali, C., Manzi, J., Katayama, M., Posnova, T., Tabernero, C., Torres, C., Verkasalo, M., Lonnqvist, J. E., Vondrakova, E., & Caprara, M. G. (2018). The contribution of religiosity to ideology: Empirical evidences from five continents. *Cross-Cultural Research, 52*(5), 524–541. https://doi.org/10.1177/1069397118774233

Caputo, J. D., Vattimo, G., & Robbins, J. W. (2007). *After the death of god.* Columbia University Press.

Carlson, R. (1971). Where is the person in personality research? *Psychological Bulletin, 75,* 203–219.

Choi, K.-H., Wojcicki, J., & Valencia-Garcia, D. (2004). Introducing and negotiating the use of female condoms in sexual relationships: Qualitative interviews with women attending a family planning clinic. *AIDS and Behavior, 8*(3), 251–261. https://doi.org/10.1023/B:AIBE.0000044073.74932.6f

Čierna, A. (2021a). *Diskurz o sexualite u detí v mladšom školskom veku. (Discourse on sexuality in children aged 6-10 years).* [Master Thesis, Comenius University, Bratislava].

Čierna, A. (2021b). Je, aj keď nie je: o implicitnosti sexuálnej výchovy. [Is, even if is not: On the implicitness of sexual education]. In M. Baránková (Ed.), *Community psychology in Slovakia 2021: Proceedings from 8th conference* (pp. 53–71). Institute of Applied Psychology, Comenius University in Bratislava.

Čonková, Ľ. (2004). Rómske dieťa ako sociálne znevýhodnené na prahu školy. *Naša škola, 8*(3), 22–29.

Crompton, S. (2002). French lessons in amorality. *Daily Telegraph, June, 5,* 2002.

Curt, B. C. (1994). *Textuality and tectonics: Troubling social and psychological science.* Open University Press.

Dalrymple, W. (2009). *Nine lives: In search of the sacred in modern India.* Bloomsbury.

Danziger, K. (1997). *Naming the mind: How psychology found its language.* London: SAGE.

Davidson, D. (1971). Agency. In B. W. Bronaugh, R. N. Bronaugh, & A. Marras (Eds.), *Agent, action, and reason* (pp. 1–26). University of Toronto Press.

De Bro, S. C., Campbell, S. M., & Peplau, L. A. (1994). Influencing a partner to use a condom: A college student perspective. *Psychology of Women Quarterly, 18*(2), 165–182. https://doi.org/10.1111/j.1471-6402.1994.tb00449.x

Dean-Jones, L. (1992). The politics of pleasure: Female sexual appetite in the Hippocratic corpus. In D. C. Stanton (Ed.), *Discourses of sexuality. From Aristotle to AIDS* (pp. 48–78). The University of Michigan Press.

Deleuze, G., & Guattari, F. (1987). *A thousand plateaus: Capitalism and schizophrenia.* University of Minnesota Press.

Diehl, S. (2011, October 31). *Abortion cemocracy: Poland/South Africa deutsche Untertitel Teil 1* [Video]. YouTube. https://www.youtube.com/watch?v=mfNp4UxtrQI

Domínguez, G. E., Pujol, J., Motzkau, J. F., & Popper, M. (2017). Suspended transitions and affective orderings: From troubled monogamy to liminal polyamory. *Theory & Psychology, 27*(2), 183–197. https://doi.org/10.1177/09593 54317700289

Eagly, A. H., & Wood, W. (1999). The origins of sex differences in human behavior: Evolved dispositions versus social roles. *American Psychologist, 54*(6), 408–423. https://doi.org/10.1037/0003-066X.54.6.408

Eisler, A. D., Wester, M., Yoshida, M., & Bianchi, G. (1999). Attitudes, beliefs, and opinions about suicide: A cross-cultural comaprison of Sweden, Japan, and Slovakia. In J. C. Lasry, J. Adair, & K. Dion (Eds.), *Latest contributions to cross-cultural psychology.* Swets and Zeitlinger.

Ellis, A. (1970). *Ako milovať.* Smena.

Elms, A. C. (1975). The crisis of confidence in social psychology. *American Psychologist, 30,* 967–976.

Erikson, E. H. (1968). Identity: Youth and crisis.

Evans, D. (1993). *T. Sexual citizenship.* Routledge.

Farberow, N. L. (1973). The crisis is chronic. *American Psychologist, 28,* 388–394.

Fahs, B., & McClelland, S. I. (2016). When sex and power collide: An argument for critical sexuality studies. *The Journal of Sex Research, 53*(4-5), 392–416.

Feeney, J. A. (1994). Attachment style, communication patterns, and satisfaction across the life cycle of marriage. *Personal Relationships, 1*(4), 333–348. https://doi.org/10.1111/j.1475-6811.1994.tb00069.x

Feyerabend, P. (2010). *Against method.* VERSO. (Original work published 1975.).

Fileborn, B., Brown, G., Lyons, A., Hinchliff, S., Heywood, W., Minichiello, V., Malta, S., Barrett, C., & Crameri, P. (2018). Safer sex in later life: Qualitative interviews with older Australians on their understandings and practices of safer sex. *The journal of Sex Research, 55*(2), 164–177.

Fischer, R. (2012). Value isomorphism in the European Social Survey: Exploration of meaning shifts in values across levels. *Journal of Cross-Cultural Psychology, 43*(6), 883–898. https://doi.org/10.1177/0022022111413276

Fiske, D. W. (1974). The limits for the conventional science of personality. *Journal of personality, 42,* 1–11.

Flowers, P., Smith, J. H., Sheeran, P., & Beail, N. (1997). Identities and gay mens sexual decision-making. In P. Aggleton, P. davies, & H. Graham (Eds.), *AIDS, Activism and Alliances* (pp. 192–213). London: Francis and Taylor.

Forrester, J. W. (1971). *World dynamics*. Wright-Allen Press.

Foucault, M. (1979). The history of sexuality. In: *An introduction* (Vol. 1). Allen Lane.

Foucault, M. (1990). The history of sexuality. In: *The care of the self* (Vol. 3). Pengiun Books.

Foucault, M. (1992). The history of sexuality. In: *The use of pleasure* (reprinted) (Vol. 2). Penguin Books.

Foucault, M. (1998). *Ethics: Subjectivity and Ttruth*. The New Press.

Foucault, M. (2000). Technológie seba samého. In M. Foucault (Ed.), *Moc, subjekt a sexualita: Výber z článkov a rozhovorov publikovaných v rokoch 1980-1988*. [Power, subject and sexuality: a selection of articles and interviews published 1980-1988]. (M. Marcelli, Trans.). pp. 186–214. Kalligram. (Original work published 1988).

Fraser, N. (2007). *Rozvíjení radikální imaginace: Globální přerozdelování, uznání a rerezentace*. Filosofia.

Fraser, N., & Honneth, A. (2004). *Přerozdělování nebo uznání?* Filosofia.

Freud, S. (1896). *The Aetiology of Hysteria*. http://staferla.free.fr/Freud/ Freud%20complete%20Works.pdf, pp. 170–180. accessed November 17, 2022.

Freud, S. (1990). *O člověku a kultuře*. Odeon.

Frie, R. (2008a). *Psychological agency: Theory, practice, and culture*. Bradford Book.

Frie, R. (2008b). Introduction: The situated nature of psychological agency. In R. Frie (Ed.), *Psychological agency: Theory, practice, and culture* (pp. 1–32).

Frosh, S. (2002). *After words*. Palgrave.

Fukuyama, F. (2018). *Identity: The demand for dignity and the politics of resentment*. Farrar.

Gagnon, J. H., & Parker, R. G. (1995). Conceiving sexuality. In R. G. Parker & J. H. Gagnon (Eds.), *Conceiving sexuality – approaches to sex research in a postmodern world* (pp. 3–18). Routledge.

Gangestad, S. W., & Simpson, J. A. (2000). The evolution of human mating: Trade-offs and strategic pluralism. *Behavioral and Brain Sciences, 23*(4), 573–587. https://doi.org/10.1017/S0140525X0000337X

Gergen, K. (1998). The ordinary, the original, and the believable in psychology's construction of the person. In B. M. Bayer & J. Shotter (Eds.), *Reconstructing the psychological subject: Bodies, practices and technologies* (pp. 111–125). SAGE Publications.

Giddens, A. (1992). *The transformation of intimacy: Sexuality, love and eroticism in modern societies*. Polity Press.

Gill, R. (2003a). Discourse analysis. In M. W. Bauer & G. Gaskell (Eds.), *Qualitative research* (pp. 172–191). Sage Publications.

Gill, R. (2003b). Power and the production of subjects: A genealogy of the new man and the new lad. *The Sociological Review, 51*(1), 34–56.

Gilligan, C. (1982). *In a different voice: Psychological theory and women's development.* Harvard University Press.

Golombok, S., & Rust, J. (1983). *Golombok Rust inventory of sexual satisfaction.* International Society for Research on Sexual Education.

Gondec, M., & Bianchi, G. (2012). Minoritné diskurzy zvádzania. *Psychológia a patopsychológia dieťaťa, 46*(4), 287–314.

Gouldner, A. W. (1970). *The coming crisis of Western sociology.* New York: Basic Books.

Grass, G. (1978). *The flounder* (1st ed.). Harcourt Brace Jovanovich.

Greco, M., & Stenner, P. (2008). *Emotions: A social science reader.* Routledge.

Greco, M., & Stenner, P. (2017). From paradox to pattern shift: Conceptualising liminal hotspots and their affective dynamics. *Theory & Psychology, 27*(2), 147–166.

Haavio-Mannila, E., Ross, J. P., & Kontula, O. (1997). Repression, revolution, and ambivalence: The sexual life of three generations. *Acta Sociologica, 39,* 409–430.

Hallway, W. (1998). Gender difference and the production of subjectivity. In J. Henriques, W. Hollway, C. Urwin, C. Venn, & V. Walkerdine (Eds.), *Changing the subject: Psychology, social regulation and subjectivit* (pp. 223–262). Routledge.

Han, B. C. (2016). *Vyhořelá společnost.* Rybka Publishers.

Häusslers, J. (1826). *Ueber die Beziehungen des Sexualsystems zur Psyche ueberhaupt und zum Kretenismus im Besonderen.* Würzburg.

Henriques, J., Hollway, W., Urwin, C., Venn, C., & Walkerdine, V. (2005). *Changing the subject. Psychology, social regulation and subjectivity.* London: Routledge.

Holzkamp, K. (1991). Societal and individual life processes. In C. W. Tolman & W. Maiers (Eds.), *Critical psychology. Contributions to an historical science of the subject* (pp. 50–64). Cambridge University Press.

Hubert, M. (1998). Studying and comapring sexual behaviour and HIV/AIDS in Europe. In M. Hubert, N. Bajos, & T. Sandfort (Eds.), *Sexual behaviour and HIV/AIDS in Europe* (pp. 3–36). UCL Press.

Hymes, D. (Ed.). (1972). *Reinventing anthropology.* New York: Pantheon.

Ingham, R., Jaramazovic, E., Stevens, D., Van Wesenbeeck, I., & Van Zessen, G. (1996). *Protocol for comparative qualitative studies on sexual conduct and HIV risks.* Centre for Sexual Health Research.

Irwin, A., & Michael, M. (2003). *Science, social theory and public knowledge.* Open University Press.

Jankuv, J. (2006). Medzinárodné a európske mechanizmy ochrany ľudských práv [International and European mechanisms of protection of human rights]. Bratislava: Iura Edition.

Jodelet, D. (2008). Social representations: The beautiful invention. *Journal for the Theory of Social Behaviour, 38*(4), 411–430.

Johansson, T. (2007). *The transformation of sexuality: Gender and identity in contemporary youth culture.* Ashgate.

Kaan, H. (1844). *Psychopathia Sexualis.* Apud Leopoldum Voss.

Katz, J. (2007). *The invention of heterosexuality.* University of Chicago Press.

Kelly, M. (2007). *The seven levels of intimacy: The art of loving and the joy of being loved.* Simon and Schuster.

Kerlinger, F. N. (1972). *Základy výzkumu chování.* Academia.

Kitzinger, C. (1987). *The social construction of lesbianism.* Sage Publications.

Kleinman, A., & Fitz–Henry, E. (2007). The experiential basis of subjectivity. How individuals change in the context of societal transformation. In J. Biel, B. Good, & A. Kleinman (Eds.), *Subjectivity: Ethnographic investigations* (pp. 53–65). University of California Press.

Kline, A., Kline, E., & Oken, E. (1992). Minority women and sexual choice in the age of AIDS. *Social Science & Medicine, 34*(4), 447–457. https://doi.org/10.1016/0277-9536(92)90305-A

Knapp, J., Zeratsky, J., & Kowitz, B. (2016). *Sprint: How to solve big problems and test new ideas in just five days.* Bantam Press.

Kolm, C. (2003). Politisk lesbisk i senmodern tid. In T. Johansson & P. Lalander (Eds.), *Sexualitetens omvandlilngar. Politisk lesbiskhet, unga kristna ochmachokulturen.* Daidalos.

Kövérová, E. (2016). Školy ako pozitívne deviantné systémy [Schools as positively deviant systems]. *PEDAGOGIKA.SK, 7*(2), 77–102.

Kövérová, E. (2021). Conditions for school success of young people from marginalized Roma communities in Slovakia - Looking for positive deviance practices. *Positivedeviance.org/case-studies.* https://positivedeviance.org/case-studiesall/2021/1/4/conditions-for-school-success-of-young-people-frommarginalized-roma-communities-mrc-in-slovakia-looking-for-positive-deviance-practices, accessed November 17, 2022.

Krahé, B., Bieneck, S., & Scheinberger-Olwig, R. (2007a). The role of sexual scripts in sexual aggression and victimization. *Archives of Sexual Behavior, 36*(5), 687–701. https://doi.org/10.1007/s10508-006-9131-6

Krahé, B., Bieneck, S., & Scheinberger-Olwig, R. (2007b). Adolescents' sexual scripts: Schematic representations of consensual and nonconsensual heterosexual interactions. *Journal of Sex Research, 44*(4), 316–327. https://doi.org/10.1080/00224490701580923

Krahe, B., Berger, A., Vanwesenbeeck, I., Bianchi, G., Chliaoutakis, J., Fernandez-Fuertes, A. A., Fuertes, A., de Matos, M. G., Hadjigeorgiou, E., Haller, B.,

Hellemans, S., Izdebski, Z., Kouta, C., Meijnckens, D., Murauskiene, L., Papadakaki, M., Ramiro, L., Reis, M., Symons, K., Tomaszewska, P., Vicario-Molina, I., & Zygadlo, A. (2015). Prevalence and correlates of young people's sexual aggression perpetration and victimisation in 10 European countries: A multi-level analysis. *Culture Health & Sexuality, 17*(6), 682–699. https://doi.org/10.1080/13691058.2014.989265

Krahe, B., de Haas, S., Vanwesenbeeck, I., Bianchi, G., Chliaoutakis, J., Fuertes, A., de Matos, M. G., Hadjigeorgiou, E., Hellemans, S., Kouta, C., Meijnckens, D., Murauskiene, L., Papadakaki, M., Ramiro, L., Reis, M., Symons, K., Tomaszewska, P., Vicario-Molina, I., & Zygadlo, A. (2016). Interpreting survey questions about sexual aggression in cross-cultural research: A qualitative study with young adults from nine European countries. *Sexuality and Culture, 20*(1), 1–23. https://doi.org/10.1007/s12119-015-9321-2

Krajčovičová, M. (2009). Kultúra, kompetencie a sociokultúrne špecifiká Rómov = Culture and socio-cultural characteristics of Romany (Gypsy). In I. Kovalčíková (Ed.), *Kultúra a kompetencie: Adaptívne schopnosti rómskych žiakov* (pp. 38–63). Prešovská univerzita.

Kuhn, T. S. (1970/1996). *The structure of scientific revolution.* University of Chicago Press.

Lacan, J. (2006). *Le Séminaire XVI: D'un autre à l'Autre Broché.* Le Seuil.

Laplanche, J. (1999). *Entre séduction et inspiration: L'homme* (1st ed.) Presses universitaires de France.

Lawson, B. (1980). *How designers think: The design process demystified.* Architectural Press.

Lee, A. J. (2015). Integrating subjects: Linking surveillance experiences to social patterns using ethno-epistemic assemblages. *Surveillance & Society, 13*(3/4), 385–399. https://doi.org/10.24908/ss.v13i3/4.5402

Lees, S. (1993). *Sugar and spice: Sexuality and adolescent girls.* Penguin books.

Lester, D., & Bean J. (1992). Attribution of causes to suicide. *Journal of Social Psychology, 132,* 679–680.

Lewis, J. (2001). *The end of marriage?* Edward Elgar.

Libby, R. W., & Straus, M. A. (1980). Make love not war? Sex, sexual meanings, and violence in a sample of university students. *Archives of Sexual Behavior, 9*(2), 133–148. https://doi.org/10.1007/BF01542265

Liégeois, J.-P. (1997). Rómovia, Cigáni, kočovníci. Rada Európy.

Luhmann, N. (1986). *Love as passion: The codification of intimacy.* Harvard University Press.

Laumann, E. O., Gagnon, J. H., Michael, R. T., & Michaels, S. (1996). The Social Organization of Sexuality: Sexual Practices in the United States. *American Journal of Public Health, 86*(7), 1037–1039.

Lukšík, I. (2003). Interaction of sexual and drugs risks: Summarisation of results from two sociocultural. *Československá psychologie, 47*(5), 437–450.

Lukšík, I. (2013). *Faktorové zobrazenie ľudskej subjektivity.* Pedagogická fakulta Trnavskej univerzity v Trnave.

Lukšík, I., Bianchi, G., Popper, M., & Supeková, M. (1998). Interakcia drogových a sexuálnych rizík mladých ľudí na Slovensku. In V. Mayer, P. Duchaj, & A. Zachová (Eds.), *Prevencia HIV/AIDS: nové príklady a rozhodovacie factory* (pp. 89–95). Liga proti AIDS.

Machovec, M. (1998). *Filosofie tváří v tvář zániku* (1st ed.). Akropolis.

MacMurray, J. (1957). *The self as sgent.* Faber & Faber.

Maffesoli, M. (1993). *The shadow of Dionysus: A contribution to the sociology of the orgy.* State University of New York Press.

Maffesoli, M. (1996). *The time of the tribes the decline of individualism in mass society.* SAGE Publications Ltd.

Maffesoli, M. (2006). *Rytmus života: Variáce o postmodenom imaginárne.* SOFA.

Maffesoli, M. (2012, March 23). *Sociálna erotika* [Video]. YouTube. https://www.youtube.com/watch?v=BuA29YFOJv4

Maffesoli, M. (2014). *Postmoderné emocionálne spoločenstvá* [Postmodern emotional associations]. Lecture.

Maierhofer, W. (2017). Abortion cemocracy: Sarah Diehl's advocacy documentary film for women's rights in Poland and South Africa. *Research ArticleSexual Health Issues, 1*(1), 1–7.

Maiers, W. (1991). Critical psychology: Historical background and task Wolfgang Maiers. In C. W. Tolman & W. Maiers (Eds.), *Critical psychology. Contributions to an historical science of the subject* (pp. 23–49). Cambridge University Press.

Mann, A. B. (1990). Výber manželského partnera u Cigánov-Rómov na Spiši (k problematike existencie "cigánskej skupiny"). *Slovenský národopis, 38*(1-2), 278–284.

Marshall, T. H. (1950). *Citizenship and social class and other essays.* Cambridge University Press.

Martin, J., Sugarman, J., & Thompson, J. (2003). *Psychology and the question of agency.* SUNY Press.

Masaryk, R., Lášticová, B., Bačová, V., Bianchi, G., Čermák, I., Miovský, M., & Plichtová, J. (2017). Etablovanie z nás nesníma zodpovednosť: prísluby a súčasnosť kvalitatívneho výskumu v Čechách a na Slovensku. *Československá psychologie, 61*(4), 401–414.

Máthé, R., & Ritomský, L. (2004). Iniciálne sexuálne aktivity v podmienkach Slovenska. *Sexuológia, 4*, 15–20.

Meadows, D. H. (2008). *Thinking in systems.* Earthscan.

Meadows, D. H., Meadows, D. L., Randers, J., & Behrens, W. W., III. (1972). *The limits to growth. A report for the club of Rome's project on the predicament of mankind.* Universe Books.

Mogilski, J. (2021). *Willingness to engage in consensual non-monogamy is greater among those for whom mate switching is favorable.* Paper presented at the 32nd International Congress of Psychology, Prague.

Moscovici, S. (1961). *La psychanalyse, son image et son public.* Presses Universitaires de France.

Moscovici, S. (2001). Why a Theory of social representations. In K. Deaux & G. Philogene (Eds.), *Representations of the social. Brindging theoretical traditions* (pp. 18–61). Blackwell.

Moret, L. B., Glaser, B. A., Page, R. C., & Bergeron, E. F. (1998). Intimacy and sexual satisfaction in unmarried couple relationships: A pilot study. *Family Journal, 6,* 33–39.

Murstein, B. I., & Tuerkheimer, A. (1998). Gender differences in love, sex, and motivation for sex. *Psychological Reports, 82*(2), 435–450. https://doi.org/10.2466/pr0.1998.82.2.435

Nagel, T. (2014). What is it like to be a bat? *The Philosophical Review, 83,* 425–450.

Neely-Barnes, S. (2010). Latent class models in social work. *Social Work Research, 34*(2), 114–121. https://doi.org/10.1093/swr/34.2.114

O'Neill, O. (1990). Practices of toleration. In J. Lichtenberg (Ed.), *Democracy and the mass media* (1st ed., pp. 155–185). Cambridge University Press. https://doi.org/10.1017/CBO9781139172271.007

Olmstead, S. B., Billen, R. M., Conrad, K. A., Pasley, K., & Fincham, F. D. (2013). Sex, commitment, and casual sex relationships among college men: A mixed-methods analysis. *Archives of Sexual Behavior, 42*(4), 561–571. https://doi.org/10.1007/s10508-012-0047-z

Olmstead, S. B., Conrad, K. A., & Anders, K. M. (2018). First semester college students' definitions of and expectations for engaging in hookups. *Journal of Adolescent Research, 33*(3), 275–305.

Olsen, W. (2007). Critical realist explorations in methodology. *Methodological Innovations Online, 2*(2), 1–5.

Olsen, W. (2012). *Data collection.* SAGE.

Oosterhuis, H. (2012). Sexual modernity in the works of Richard von Krafft-Ebing and Albert Moll. *Medical History, 56*(2), 133–155. https://doi.org/10.1017/mdh.2011.30

Parker, I. (1989). *The crisis in modern social psychology and how to end it.* Routledge.

Parker, I. (2002). *Critical discursive psychology.* Palgrave.

Patomäki, H., & Wight, C. (2000). After postpositivism? The promises of critical realism. *International Studies Quarterly, 44*(2), 213–237.

Patterson, C. H. (1980). *Theories of counseling and psychotherapy.* Harper & Row.

Plummer, K. (1995). *Telling sexual stories: Power, change, and social worlds.* Routledge.

Plummer, K. (2003). *Intimate citizenship: Private decisions and public dialogues.* University of Washington Press.

Popper, M., Bianchi, G., & Lukšík, I. (1997). Sociálne ospravedlnenia rizikového sexuálneho správania. In I. Sarmány-Schuller, M. Kočš, & E. Jaššová (Eds.), *Človek na počiatku nového tisícročia* (pp. 109–111). Slovenská psychologická spoločnosť.

Popper, M., Bianchi, G., Lukšík, I., Supeková, M., & Ingham, R. (2005). The social context of sexual health among young people in Slovakia: Comparisons with the United Kingdom and the Netherlands. In A. Štulhofer & T. Sandfort (Eds.), *Sexuality and gender in postcommunist Europe and Russia* (pp. 365–390). Haworth Press.

Popper, M., Bianchi, G., Szeghy, P., & Lukšík, I. (2006). Constructions of gender in partnership narratives. *Human Affairs, 16*(2), 144–159.

Potter, J. (2003). Discursive psychology: Between method and paradigm. *Discourse & Society, 14*(6), 783–794.

Potter, J., Wetherell, M., Gill, R., & Edwards, D. (1990). Discourse: Noun, verb or social practice? *Philosophical Psychology, 3*(2–3), 205–217. https://doi.org/10.1080/09515089008572999

Powell, A. (2010). *Sex, power and consent: Youth culture and the unwritten rules.* University Press.

Prager, K. J. (1995). *The psychology of intimacy.* Guilford Press.

Rey, F. G. (2017). The topic of subjectivity in psychology: Contradictions, paths and new alternatives. *Journal for the Theory of Social Behaviour, 47*(4), 502–521.

Reynolds, P. (2010). Disentangling privacy and intimacy: Intimate citizenship, private boundaries and public transgressions. *Human Affairs, 20*(1), 33–42. https://doi.org/10.2478/v10023-010-0004-1

Roberts, M. J. (1974). On the nature and condition of social science. *Daedalus, 103*(3), 47–64.

Rorty, R., & Vattimo, G. (2007). Budoucnost náboženství. Karolinum.

Roseneil, S. (2006). On not living with a partner: Unpicking coupledom and cohabitation. *Sociological Research Online, 11*(3), 111–124. https://doi.org/10.5153/sro.1413

Rošková, V., Rosová, E., & Bianchi, G. (1998). Kvalitatívna analýza vnímania rizika deťmi a adolescentami. *Psychológia a patopsychológia dieťaťa, 33*(3), 203–216.

Rosová, V., Bianchi, G., & Sládeková, L. (1989). Environment in the paradigm of psychological space. *Československa Psychologie, 33*(6), 559–579.

Rosová, V., Rošková, E., & Bianchi, G. (1996). Percepcia rizík vo výberoch detskej populácie na Slovensku. *Acta Environmentalica Universitatis Comenianae, 8*, 77–87.

Rushdie, S. (2021). *Languages of truth.* Jonathan Cape.

Saalfield, C. (1993). Lesbian marriage... (k)not! In A. Stein (Ed.), *Sisters, sexperts, queers: Beyond the lesbian nation* (pp. 187–195). Penguin.

Sábato, E. (2002). *Spisovatel a jeho přízraky.* Mladá fronta.

Scarfone, D. (2001). Entre séduction et inspiration: L'homme, de Jean Laplanche, Paris, PUF, coll. "Quadrige", 1999, 338 pages. *Santé Mentale au Québec*, *26*(1), 297. https://doi.org/10.7202/014522ar

Schmitt, D. P., Alcalay, L., Allik, J., Ault, L., Austers, I., Bennett, K. L., Bianchi, G., Boholst, F., Cunen, M. A. B., Braeckman, J., Brainerd, E. G., Caral, L. G. A., Caron, G., Casullo, M. M., Cunningham, M., Daibo, I., De Backer, C., De Souza, E., Diaz-Loving, R., et al. (2003a). Universal sex differences in the desire for sexual variety: Tests from 52 nations, 6 continents, and 13 islands. *Journal of Personality and Social Psychology*, *85*(1), 85–104. https://doi.org/10.1037/0022-3514.85.1.85

Schmitt, D. P., Alcalay, L., Allensworth, M., Allik, J., Ault, L., Austers, I., Bennett, K. L., Bianchi, G., Boholst, F., Cunen, M. A. B., Braekman, J., Brainerd, E. G., Caral, L. G. A., Caron, G., Casullo, M. M., Cunningham, M., Daibo, I., De Backer, C., De Souza, E., et al. (2003b). Are men universally more dismissing than women? Gender differences in romantic attachment across 62 cultural regions. *Personal Relationships*, *10*(3), 307–331. https://doi.org/10.1111/1475-6811.00052

Schmitt, D. P., Diniz, G., Alcalay, L., Durkin, K., Allensworth, M., Echegaray, M., Allik, J., Eremsoy, E., Ault, L., Euler, H. A., Austers, I., Falzon, R., Bennett, K. L., Fisher, M. L., Bianchi, G., Foley, D., Boholst, F., Fowler, R., Cunen, M. A. B., et al. (2004a). Patterns and universals of adult romantic attachment across 62 cultural regions – are models of self and of other pancultural constructs? *Journal of Cross-Cultural Psychology*, *35*(4), 367–402. https://doi.org/10.1177/0022022104266105

Schmitt, D. P., Alcalay, L., Allik, J., Angleitner, A., Ault, L., Austers, I., Bennett, K. L., Bianchi, G., Boholst, F., Cunen, M. A. B., Braeckman, J., Brainerd, E. G., Caral, L. G. A., Caron, G., Casullo, M. M., Cunningham, M., Daibo, I., De Backer, C., De Souza, E., Diaz-Loving, R., et al. (2004b). Patterns and universals of mate poaching across 53 nations: The effects of sex, culture, and personality on romantically attracting another person's partner. *Journal of Personality and Social Psychology*, *86*(4), 560–584. https://doi.org/10.1037/0022-3514.86.4.560

Schwartz, S. H. (1992). Universals in the content and structure of values: Theoretical advances and empirical tests in 20 countries. In M. P. Zanna (Ed.), *Advances in experimental social psychology* (Vol. 25, pp. 1–65). Academic Press. https://doi.org/10.1016/S0065-2601(08)60281-6

Schwartz, S. H. (1994). Beyond individualism/collectivism: New cultural dimensions of values. In U. Kim, H. C. Triandis, Ç. Kâğitçibaşi, S.-C. Choi, & G. Yoon (Eds.), *Individualism and collectivism: Theory, method, and applications* (pp. 85–119). Sage Publications.

Schwartz, S. H. (1999). A theory of cultural values and some implications for work. *Applied Psychology: An International Review, 48*(1), 23–47. https://doi.org/10.1111/j.1464-0597.1999.tb00047.x

Schwartz, S. H. (2012). An overview of the schwartz theory of basic values. *Online Readings in Psychology and Culture, 2*(1). https://doi.org/10.9707/2307-0919.1116

Schwartz, S. H., Bardi, A., & Bianchi, G. (2000). Value adaptation to the imposition and collapse of communist regimes in East-Central Europe. In S. A. Renshon & J. Duckitt (Eds.), *Political psychology: Cultural and crosscultural foundations* (pp. 217–237). Macmillan Press Ltd.

Schwartz, S. H., Caprara, G. V., Vecchione, M., Bain, P., Bianchi, G., Caprara, M. G., Cieciuch, J., Kirmanoglu, H., Baslevent, C., Lonnqvist, J. E., Mamali, C., Manzi, J., Pavlopoulos, V., Posnova, T., Schoen, H., Silvester, J., Tabernero, C., Torres, C., Verkasalo, M., et al. (2014). Basic personal values underlie and give coherence to political values: A cross national study in 15 countries. *Political Behavior, 36*(4), 899–930. https://doi.org/10.1007/s11109-013-9255-z

Sennett, R. (1986). *The fall of public man.* Faber and Faber.

Simon, W. (1996). *Postmodern sexualities.* London, Routledge.

Singhal, A., & Dura, L. (2009). *Protecting Children from Exploitation and Trafficking.* Save the Children Federation.

Singhal, A., Bruscell, P., & Lindberg, C. (2010). *Inviting Everyone: Healing Healthcare through Positive Deviance.* Bordentown: Plexus Press.

Singhal, A., Greiner, K., & Dura, L. (2010). Positive Deviance makes Inroads into Health Care. In A. Singhal, P. Bruscell, & C. Lindberg (Eds.), *Inviting Everyone: Healing Healthcare through Positive Deviance,* pp. 23–36. Bordentown: Plexus Press.

Sprague, J., & Quadagno, D. (1989). Gender and sexual motivation: An exploration of two assumptions. *Journal of Psychology & Human Sexuality, 2*(1), 57–76. https://doi.org/10.1300/J056v02n01_05

Stainton, R. W. (2003). *Social psychology: Experimental and critical approaches.* Open University Press.

Stam, H. J., Lubek, I., & Radtke, H. L. (1998). Repopulating social psychology texts: Disembodied "subjects" and embodied subjectivity. In B. M. Bayer & J. Shotter (Eds.), *Reconstructing the psychological subject: Bodies, practices and technologies* (pp. 153–186). Sage Publications. https://doi.org/10.4135/9780857026019.n9

Stanton, D. C. (Ed.). (1992). *Discourses of sexuality. From Aristotle to AIDS.* The University of Michigan Press.

Starker, S. (1989). *Oracle at the supermarket; The American preoccupation with self-help books.* New Brunswick: Transaction Publishers.

Stenner, P. (2017). *Liminality and experience. A transdisciplinary approach to the psychosocial.* Palgrave Macmillan.

Stenner, P., & Clinch, M. (2013). *Thinking about affectivity and liminality together*. CCIG. Retrieved from http://www.open.ac.uk/ccig/blogs/thinking-about-affectivity-and-liminality-together

Stenner, P. H. D., Bianchi, G., Popper, M., Supeková, M., Lukšík, I., & Pujol, J. (2006). Constructions of sexual relationships – a study of the views of young people in Catalunia, England and Slovakia and their health implications. *Journal of Health Psychology, 11*(5), 669–684. https://doi.org/10.1177/1359105306066617

Stephenson, W. (1953). *The study of behavior*. University of Chicago Press.

Sterman, J. D. (1991). A skeptic's guide to computer models. In G. O. Barney, W. B. Kreutzer, M. J. Garrett, & W. B. Kreutzer (Eds.), *Managing anation: The microcomputer software catalog* (pp. 209–229). Westview Press.

Strachey, J. (1962). *The standard edition of the complete psychological works of Sigmund Freud, Volume III (1893-1899): Early psycho-analytic publications* (pp. i–vi). The Hogarth Press.

Strauss, A., & Corbin, J. (1994). Grounded theory methodology: An overview. In N. Denzin & Y. Lincoln (Eds.), *Handbook of qualitative research* (pp. 273–284). Sage Publications.

Sugarman, J. (2008). Understanding persons as relational agents. In R. Frie (Ed.), *Psychological agency: Theory, practice, and culture* (pp. 73–94). Bradford Book.

Supeková, M., & Bianchi, G. (2000). Sexual education and satisfaction of sexually more active young people (a qualitative approach). *Československá psychologie, 44*(1), 56–76.

Supeková, M., Lukšík, I., Bianchi, G., & Popper, M. (1998). *Kulturálne aspekty sexuality v diskurze a sexuálnom správaní sa žien*. Manuscript.

Supeková, M., Bianchi, G., Popper, M., Lukšík, I., & Ingham, R. (2005). The subjective meaning of sex and sexual satisfaction among more active young adults in Slovakia. In A Štulhofer, & T. Sandfort (Eds.), *Sexuality and gender in postcommunist Europe and Russia*. Binghamton: Haworth Press, str. 263–296.

Šviráková, E., & Bianchi, G. (2018). Design thinking, grounded theory, and system dynamics modeling-an integrative methodology for social sciences and humanities. *Human Affairs-Postdisciplinary Humanities & Social Sciences Quarterly, 28*(3), 312–327. https://doi.org/10.1515/humaff-2018-0025

Taylor, S. E., Klein, L. C., Lewis, B. P., Gruenewald, T. L., Gurung, R. A., & Updegraff, J. A. (2000). Biobehavioral responses to stress in females: Tend-and-befriend, not fight-or-flight. *Psychological Review, 107*(3), 411–429. https://doi.org/10.1037/0033-295x.107.3.411

Teyssot, G. (2010). Windows and screens: A topology of the intimate and the extimate. *Log*, New York, No. 18, p. 75–88.

Tisseron, S. (2002). *L'Intimité surexposée*. Flammarion.

Tisseron, S. (2008). *Virtuel, mon amour. Penser, aimer, souffrir, à l'ère des nouvelles technologies*. A. Michel.

Tisseron, S. (2011). Intimité et extimité. *Communications, 1*(88), 83–91. https://doi.org/10.3917/commu.088.0083

Tolman, C. W. (1991). Critical psychology: An overview. In C. W. Tolman & W. Maiers (Eds.), *Critical psychology: Contributions to an historical science of the subject* (pp. 1–22). Cambridge University Press.

Trivers, R. (1972). Parental investment and sexual selection. In B. Cambell (Ed.), *Sexual selection and the descent of man, 1871-1971* (pp. 136–179). Aldine.

Turner, B. S. (2001). Outline of a general theory of cultural citizenship. In N. Stevenson (Ed.), *Culture and citizenship* (pp. 11–32). SAGE Publications Ltd. https://doi.org/10.4135/9781446217665

Valent, M. (1989). Výchova k rodičovstvu. In J. Molčan (Ed.), *Vybrané kapitoly zo sexuológie a hraničných odborov* (pp. 124–143). Osveta.

van Bertalanffy, L. (1968). *General system theory: Foundations, development, applications.* Braziller.

Van Gennep, A. (1960). *The rites of passage.* University of Chicago Press. (Original work published 1909.).

Vanwesenbeeck, I., Bekker, M., & van Lenning, A. (1998). Gender attitudes, sexual meanings, and interactional patterns in heterosexual encounters among college students in the Netherlands. *Journal of Sex Research, 35*(4), 317–327. https://doi.org/10.1080/00224499809551949

Vattimo, G. (2002). *After Christianity.* Columbia University Press.

Vecchione, M., Schwartz, S. H., Caprara, G. V., Schoen, H., Cieciuch, J., Silvester, J., Bain, P., Bianchi, G., Kirmanoglu, H., Baslevent, C., Mamali, C., Manzi, J., Pavlopoulos, V., Posnova, T., Torres, C., Verkasalo, M., Lonnqvist, J. E., Vondrakova, E., Welzel, C., & Alessandri, G. (2015). Personal values and political activism: A cross-national study. *British Journal of Psychology, 106*(1), 84–106. https://doi.org/10.1111/bjop.12067

Višňovský, E. (2009). *Človek ako homo agens.* Bratislava, Iris.

von Krafft-Ebing, R. (1886). *Psychopathia sexualis, eine klinisch-forensische Studie.* Enke. (von Krafft-Ebing, R. Psychopathia Sexualis: eine Klinisch-Forensische Studie (12th edn 1886/1965); tr. Franklin S. Klaf as Psychopathia Sexualis: With Especial Reference to the Antipathic Sexual Instinct. A Medico-Forensic Study. Arcade Publishing).

Walkerdine, V. (1996). Subjectivity and social class: New directions for feminist psychology. *Feminism and Psychology, 6*(3), 355–360.

Walkerdine, V. (2002). *Challenging subjects. Critical psychology for a New Millennium.* Palgrave.

Ward, T., & Salmon, K. (2011). The ethics of care and treatment of sex offenders. *Sexual Abuse, 23*(3), 397–413. https://doi.org/10.1177/1079063210382049

Warner, M. (1999). *The trouble with normal: Sex, politics, and the ethics of queer life.* Free Press.

Weeks, J. (2007). *The world we have won: The remaking of erotic and intimate life.* Routledge.

Weiss, P., & Zvěřina, J. (2001). *Sexuální chování v ČR: Situace a trendy.* Portál.

Weiss, P., Urbánek, V., & Procházka, I. (1996). První pohlavní styk. In *AIDS a My – AIDS a drogy: Zborník referátov z medzinárodného seminára Poděbrady 95* (pp. 75–78). Česko-slovensko-švýcarská zdravotnická společnost.

Wiedemann, P. M. (1992). Taboo, sin, risk: Changes in the social perception of hazards. In B. Ruck (Ed.), *Risk is a construct: Perceptions of risk perception* (pp. 41–63). Knesebeck.

Willig, C. (1993). *Introducing qualitative research in psychology: Adventures in theory and method.* Open University Press.

Winnicott, D. W. (1953). Transitional objects and transitional phenomena. *International Journal of Psychoanalysis, 34,* 89–97.

Wohlwill, J. F. (1973). *The study of behavioral development.* New York: Academic Press.

Yep, G. A., Lovaas, K. E., & Elia, J. P. (2007). A critical appraisal of assimiliationist and radical ideologies underlying same-sex marriage in LGBT communities in the United States. In K. Lovaas & M. M. Jenkins (Eds.), *Sexualities & communication in everyday life: A reader* (pp. 165–177). SAGE Publications.

Young, M., & Luquis, R. (1998). Correlates of sexual satisfaction in marriage. Canadian *Journal of Human Sexuality, 7,* 115–128.

Index[1]

---

[1] Note: Page numbers followed by 'n' refer to notes.

143

G. Bianchi, *Figurations of Human Subjectivity*,
https://doi.org/10.1007/978-3-031-19189-3

Printed by Printforce, the Netherlands